RAILWAY WALKS

WALES

In memory of my parents, Alan and Lilian Vinter

RAILWAY WALKS

WALES

JEFF VINTER

ALAN SUTTON PUBLISHING LIMITED

First published in the United Kingdom in 1994
Alan Sutton Publishing Limited
Phoenix Mill · Stroud · Gloucestershire

First published in the United States of America in 1994
Alan Sutton Publishing Inc.
83 Washington Street · Dover · NH 03520

British Library Cataloguing-in-Publication Data
A catalogue record for this book is available from the British Library.

ISBN 0–7509–0141–1

Library of Congress Cataloging-in-Publication Data applied for.

Cover illustrations, front: One of three tunnels on the former Welsh Highland Railway which carried this famous narrow gauge line through the Aberglaslyn Pass. 3½ miles of trackbed near Beddgelert, incorporating this and many other engineering features, are now open as a public footpath. (Author) *Rear*: This ex-Southern Railway parcels van now houses Afan Argoed Cycle Hire near Cynonville Halt on the former Rhondda & Swansea Bay Railway. Some 14 miles of disused railway in the Afan Valley have been converted into walking and cycling routes. (Author)

Typeset in 10/12 Plantin.
Typesetting and origination by
Alan Sutton Publishing Limited.
Printed in Great Britain by
The Bath Press, Avon, Bath.

CONTENTS

ACKNOWLEDGEMENTS

Many people inevitably lend a hand in a project like this, and I am particularly indebted to those who are listed below.

For accommodation: Pete and Gail Wills of Bridgend, and Maurice and Hilary Blencowe of Great Sutton.

For the loan of books: Pete Walker of Railway Ramblers, and Pete Wills. As always, the histories would have been much poorer without the help of Robert Turner and the staff of Winchester Library, while Robert Nicholas of Bridgend Library deserves a special mention for the amazing way in which he named, from memory, several valuable articles published in the *Railway Magazine* in the mid 1950s.

For photography and transport services: John Gibberd and David James. Interesting it may be, but racing up and down old railway lines is an arduous business without good company!

For background information: Mike Chown of Lonydd Glas Cymru and Harry Evans of Railway Ramblers, who acted as my eyes and ears in the valleys.

For information used in the gazetteer: the county, district, city and borough councils of Wales; the national park authorities for the Brecon Beacons, Snowdonia and the Pembrokeshire Coast; and Sustrans Ltd. I would particularly like to thank Liz Dean of Mid Glamorgan County Council and Dave Protheroe of Dare Valley Country Park, whose contributions were especially detailed and helpful.

For surveys and walk reports: Maurice and Hilary Blencowe, Paul Foley, John Gibberd and Nigel Willis, all of Railway Ramblers.

For details of local railways after closure: Derek Richardson, volunteer walks leader at the Greenfield Valley Heritage Park; Pete Jennings of Welsh Water; Steve Judd of Parc Cwm Darran; Huw Jones of Swansea City Council; John Weeks of Sirhowy Valley Country Park; Gillian Thomas of Islwyn Borough Council; Richard Beale of West Glamorgan County Council; Denise Fletcher of Ogwr Borough Council; Alastair Warrington of Regional Railways; and Andrew Gray and Pat Hart of the Merthyr & Cynon Groundwork Trust.

For public transport information: the staff of the various county council public transport sections, notably Christine Roberts (Clwyd), Malcolm Cowtan (Gwynedd), Andrea Jones (Dyfed), Mike Richardson (West Glamorgan), Mr G. Gould (Mid Glamorgan) and Ceri Edwards (South Glamorgan). Details of public transport in the Elan Valley were supplied by the staff of Llandrindod Wells Tourist Information Centre.

For my supply of forty- and fifty-year-old maps: David Archer, and for help with sketch maps of the lines today: John Fisher.

Finally, a special word of thanks to Jenny, Rosie and Heather, my wife and daughters, who probably think I am mad for undertaking this project but are much too kind to say so.

LOCATION OF WALKS

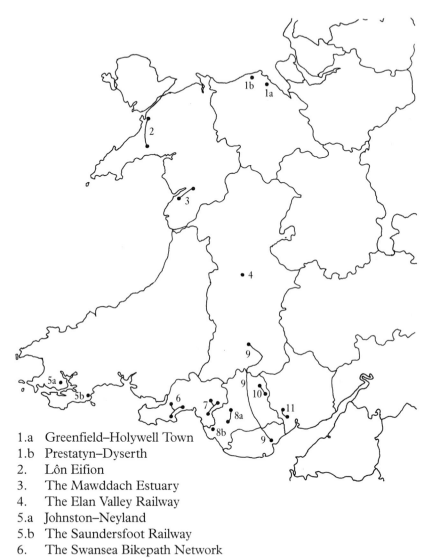

KEY TO MAPS

Railways

—————————— Railway path

- - - - - - - - - - Course of trackbed (no public access)

▪-▪-▪-▪-▪-▪-▪-▪- Operational railway

Stations

——————■—————— With buildings and platforms

——————●—————— With platforms only

——————○—————— Station site (few remains if any)

Features

—————————— Viaduct or major bridge

—)——————(— Tunnel with through access

Other Routes

══════════ Any metalled road

Note: The relevant Ordnance Survey maps are identified in the Transport and Facilities section of each chapter.

INTRODUCTION

The Victorians loved a good ruin. Crumbling castles, moss-covered mounds and the towering remains of dissolved monasteries evoked in them a particularly romantic response; and if the outline of the ruin was not quite right, they thought nothing of adjusting its appearance by the judicious removal of unwanted, protruding features. One of the ironies of living in the latter part of the twentieth century is that many of our present-day ruins were actually built by the Victorians – frequently as part of their massive and unrivalled railway system.

People often ask why I spend so much time exploring old railways, perhaps imagining that I am an incurable romantic like my Victorian predecessors. The explanation is not so simple. Certainly many old railways have an elegiac look about them, but they are also a good way of exploring the countryside, just like canals and Roman roads. What I like about them is the fact that they often choose the unexpected route – the engineer's rather than the cowherd's way, if you like – and frequently lead to little villages that have side-stepped the hustle and bustle of modern life since the last train ran, maybe thirty or more years ago. If you want to get to know the countryside, it's no good simply driving up and down trunk roads! And then there are the engineering features: stations, signal-boxes, bridges, tunnels and towering viaducts, many of them in out-of-the-way places that the common crowd never sees. Finally, if you delve into their history, you will begin to see the industries that spawned them, and to understand the forces that shaped many of our towns and cities.

Many of the earliest 'railways' in Wales were actually a by-product of the canal age. The geography and geology of the country made canal building a difficult task, so several of the canal companies' Acts authorized the construction of connecting tramways up to 8 miles from the waterway. Longer tramways might be constructed by industrialists who wanted to secure the benefits of improved transport for their factories' products. Ironically, few at the time realized that these primitive 'iron roads' contained the seed of the future, but within two or three generations, tramways had evolved into railways and the canals were eclipsed. Due to their sharp curves and steep gradients, most Welsh tramways were unsuitable for conversion into railways and a surprising number survive to this day. The Brecon Forest area is particularly rich in such remains and Stephen Hughes' authoritative book on the subject (see Bibliography) is a first rate field guide.

Tramways, then, may have become the first disused railways in Wales but they were certainly not the last. Railways came and went with the industries that spawned them and few, if any, mourned their passing. One need only look at the chequered history of the Saundersfoot Railway to see how closely some lines were linked with the vicissitudes of local industry: the 'boom and bust' turns of the economic cycle led to success and decline in equal measure. The Elan Valley Railway, which was created to build a chain of massive reservoirs in the Elan Valley west of Rhayader, was even more remarkable: it was clear from the outset that this company would exist only while the construction work was under way, but even then parts of its track were moved on a regular basis reflecting the changing needs of the building programme. This created disused railways before many locals had become aware that an operational railway existed in the first place!

The changing pattern of the railway network was a largely natural process right up until the 1950s. By this time, British Railways was pruning little-used services such as those to Blaengarw and Nantymoel, where most passengers had been lured away by rival bus operators, but there was no question of withdrawing the all-important freight trains which served the local collieries. Passenger closures began to quicken in the early 1960s as the result of further losses to bus competition and the realization that economies had to be made, but the real sea change occurred in June 1961 when Dr Richard Beeching was appointed Chairman of British Railways. In March 1963, his famous report 'The Re-Shaping of British Railways' was published and this ushered in a series of railway closures of unparalleled severity before or since. Beeching's successors adopted a similar approach and, for almost twenty years, it seemed as though an important role of railway managers was to minimize the remaining network. The contraction of the Welsh coal industry led to equal losses on the freight side, and this regrettable decline has continued right to the present day. The one hopeful sign in recent years has been the reopening of a number of valley lines such as Abercynon–Aberdare and Bridgend–Maesteg, which suggests that the closures of the Beeching and post-Beeching eras were over-zealous.

The upshot of all this has been the creation of a tremendous mileage of disused railways throughout Wales, embracing a veritable hotch-potch of tramways, standard gauge branches, former main lines, colliery railways and even the occasional privately owned system. Most of these routes have had a rum time since closure, but in the last fifteen to twenty years, many of them have been used to create off-road walks and cycle trails. The impetus for this has come from a variety of sources, not least the need to promote a healthier lifestyle, encourage environmentally-friendly tourism, and reduce our dependence on the motor car, which increasingly clogs our towns and cities while polluting the air we breathe. This, essentially, is where this book fits in, for it lists virtually every disused railway in Wales which is officially open to the public, and describes many of them in considerable detail. It is not a campaigning book, more a practical exploration of the history that lies, often undiscovered, on our own doorsteps.

By their nature, all of these walks are linear and it has been essential to include an outline of local bus services that can take you back to where you started. Due to the relatively low level of car ownership in Wales, public transport is generally excellent but a note of caution must be sounded about the local authority enquiry numbers listed in each chapter. These were set up following bus de-regulation in October 1986 and offer a first-class service for locals and visitors alike. Counties such as Clwyd and Gwynedd have taken it upon themselves to coordinate routes in a way that rival bus operators might never do themselves, and they even publish integrated county-wide timetables. Unfortunately, at the time of writing (February 1994), central government has embarked upon a review of local administration which could result in all county councils being swept away and their functions dispersed among a large number of new 'unitary authorities'. I am sorry to say that, as a result, all of these invaluable 'public transport hotlines' could cease to exist within little over a year. Assuming that this happens (although I hope it won't), I have listed the names, addresses and telephone numbers of the main bus operators in each area, who are clearly not affected by this upheaval – although they could go out of business, amalgamate with other firms, or be taken over. Without some kind of centralized information service, you simply cannot win on this one!

With regard to the railways, the consequences of impending change seem less invidious, certainly as far as they affect users of this book who are likely to be making fairly local journeys. (I am not belittling the wider problems that may occur, but they are outside the scope of this study.) While the British Rail network will probably be taken over by a number of new 'franchisees', I cannot see that they will do themselves any favours by abolishing, or even changing, the telephone enquiry numbers that in many cases passengers have used for years. Rather, I hope that they will install extra lines in order to eliminate the problems that commonly occur when one rings BR – the line permanently engaged, or the queueing system that accepts your call and then keeps you waiting for ages. Time will tell if my optimism is misplaced.

Welsh placenames are a potential minefield and I have opted for the easy solution by using the spellings given on Ordnance Survey Landranger maps. I fully recognize that some of these are wrong, but given that many readers will be using these maps in conjunction with my walk descriptions, it seemed a reasonable compromise. Ultimately, I suppose, it also deflects the blame on to someone else – perhaps no bad thing in this case. However I am reminded of an incident recounted by the railway historian Derek Barrie, whose uncle told him (roughly quoted), 'What does it matter how you spell it, boy, so long as you know where it is?'

Many of these walks now have good quality, smooth surfaces which are suitable for walking in all seasons, but do remember that the Welsh climate can be unpredictable and chillingly cold, especially on the mountains. I would think twice about going over the Brecon & Merthyr Railway's Seven Mile Bank in a T shirt and trainers, even in August. Be prepared for damp and cold weather, even when you don't expect it, and you will not come to grief. If you are cycling, please remember to sound your bell and give way to walkers, some of whom may be hard of hearing or even partially sighted; not everyone is in the first flush of youth. Be patient, be courteous.

Many cyclists are understandably concerned about the lack of safe cycling facilities in this country. If you want to do something positive about this, you can do no better than become a supporter of Sustrans, the greenways charity that has created off-road cycle trails throughout England, Scotland and Wales. All income from supporters is used to finance the initial stages of new projects which, lacking the benefit of large grants from organizations like the Countryside Commission and the Welsh Development Agency, are always the most difficult to pay for. On the other hand, if transport history appeals to you more, you might be interested in Railway Ramblers, a small national club which specializes in exploring old railways. The addresses of both these organizations are listed in Appendix A.

There is much more that could be said about disused railways generally, but the subject has been well covered in the introductions to the other three volumes in this series; so, without further ado, let the walks – and the glorious Welsh countryside – speak for themselves.

1
THE CLWYD COAST
Two Short but Steeply-Graded Branch Lines

Introduction

Anyone who has travelled by train in the West of England – especially before 1963 when Dr Beeching launched his infamous assault on the nation's railways – will be used to the idea of the main line that keeps to the high ground while throwing off branches that run downhill to the coast. Here in Clwyd, however, Welsh topography dictated a different solution, for the main line of the Chester & Holyhead Railway keeps to the coast while leaving its branches to do all the hard work. And hard work it was too: the tiny Holywell branch, while only 1¾ miles long, was built with a ruling gradient of 1 in 27, and enthusiasts visited it largely for the spectacle of a little Webb tank engine working its heart out on the steeply graded climb to its destination.

The second of the two branches described in this chapter is the short route from Prestatyn to Dyserth, once the home of LNWR 'railmotors' and a string of rail-level halts. The gradient here – never worse than 1 in 45 – seems quite innocuous when compared with that on the Holywell branch, but it could still produce clouds of exhaust from a well-loaded railmotor. Nowadays, one can enjoy the views from the line at a more leisurely pace: northwards over the coastal plain and Prestatyn, and southwards to the Clwydian Mountains. The rugged scenery to the east anticipates what will be seen from many other walks in this book, and it certainly whetted my appetite for what lay ahead. The Welsh landscape is never less than attractive, and frequently majestic: what better place to spend a walking or cycling holiday?

History

A. Greenfield to Holywell

The benefits of rail travel were first made available to the residents of Holywell when the Chester & Holyhead Railway opened its main line from Saltney Junction (2 miles west of Chester) to Bangor on 1 May 1848. Unfortunately, the station it provided for the town was actually in Greenfield, some 1½ miles to the north, and access involved a steep descent of nearly 550 ft from Halkyn Mountain, on which Holywell is perched.

Things were rather different for freight traffic, for the Holywell Limestone Co. had built a 3 ft gauge tramway some years earlier to transport lead and limestone from the mountainside above the town to the small harbour at Greenfield. This primitive line crossed the C&HR on the level just east of Holywell station and was seen as the obvious means of providing rail access to the town. Accordingly, the Holywell Railway received its Act on 29 July 1864. This authorized a 2 mile line on the course of the tramway from Holywell to a new pier at Greenfield, with a connection laid in to the C&HR at its main line station. The troublesome level crossing was to be replaced by a new bridge. In 1865, the company sought powers to construct an extension to Nannerch some 4½ miles to the south (the idea was to divert Wrexham coal to Holywell Harbour), but its proposals were defeated in Parliament by the LNWR, which by this time had purchased the impecunious Chester & Holyhead company.

The rebuilt line was opened in June 1867, complete with the promised bridge which enabled the earlier level crossing to be dismantled. The following year, the LNWR agreed to the HR constructing a platform adjacent to its main line station, but despite the opportunity to encourage passenger traffic, the local company insisted on running its line as a mineral tramway until, by the 1870s, it was neglected and disused. In 1873, it seemed that the line might be involved in one of two larger schemes backed by the GWR, but Euston saw them off in Parliament. One of these, for a Liverpool & North Wales Railway, proposed a line from Birkenhead across the Dee to the HR at Greenfield – an attempt to imitate the failed Parkgate, Chester & Birkenhead Junction Railway (see *Railway Walks: LMS*) which had proposed a line along a similar route in 1846. Having failed to become part of a larger project which might have revived it, the Holywell Railway duly went bankrupt in 1874.

In 1891, the LNWR made a surprise move and purchased the company, by which time its line was in a sorry state. It is difficult to explain why Euston made this acquisition, for it seems that it had no immediate use for it; it is not until 1902 that we read of plans for an electric tramway along the

A postcard illustrating St Winefride's Halt on the short Holywell Town branch. Note the checkrails on the inside of the curve leading to the terminus, which was just under ½ a mile distant. This view is now obscured by trees, which is a pity as the surrounding countryside is still very attractive

David Wilkes

route, although these came to nothing. The line was finally revived, oddly enough, by motor buses: on 5 June 1905, the LNWR introduced a railway bus service between Connahs Quay, Flint, Northop and Mold, and so successful was this that it introduced a similar service between Holywell station and town on 11 October the same year. The Holywell buses were so well used that the railway decided to rebuild the branch line, and two Acts were duly obtained in 1906 and 1907 authorizing alterations to the route and a new curve at Greenfield. Despite this, construction was very slow and the 1¾ mile branch was not finally opened until 1 July 1912. Apart from the two terminal stations, there was an intermediate halt at St Winefride's, a quarter of a mile from Holywell.

The passenger service at opening was very generous, with 16 return workings daily except Sundays. By 1922, the number of trains had risen to 19 daily, and by World War II, there were 29 return journeys on Saturdays and 17 on Sundays – a lavish timetable by any standards. Due to the steep gradient, trains were always worked with the engine at the bottom end of the slope, a safety precaution in case of runaways. Unfortunately, after World

War II the line became an early victim of road competition and all services were withdrawn on 6 September 1954. A quarter mile stub at the Greenfield end remained open to serve a textile factory at Crescent Siding, but this too was closed on 11 August 1957.

B. Prestatyn to Dyserth

The opening of the Chester & Holyhead Railway in 1848 and the Vale of Clwyd Railway ten years later placed the industries around Dyserth at a disadvantage, for unlike their competitors which now had easy access to rail transport, they were still lumbered with the local roads – at least as far as the nearest station. As a result, a public meeting was held on 17 November 1860 to consider a privately funded railway from Prestatyn to Dyserth and Cwm. The final form of this scheme was revealed on 28 November 1863, when plans for the line were deposited with the Clerk of the Peace at Mold.

The map of the route looked rather like a hangman's noose, which is rather appropriate when one considers its subsequent lack of success: it ran south from Prestatyn to Dyserth before describing a huge loop which rejoined the outward course some 3½ miles later. Of course, there was nothing wrong with the idea of a return loop in principal and, in different circumstances, it might have done much to simplify operations; but this particular loop involved gradients as steep as 1 in 3.8, not to mention some improbable curves, the tightest of which was of 2 chains radius. (It would be interesting to know how the promoters thought they could operate such a railway safely.) To their credit, the loop was dropped leaving only the Prestatyn–Dyserth section, but for some reason the entire project was abandoned before it could start its passage through Parliament.

Scenting some profitable and untapped traffic, the LNWR stepped in two years later when it deposited plans for its own Prestatyn & Cwm Railway which, despite the title, proposed a line that would run no further south than Dyserth. This duly received its Act on 16 July 1866. Surveying work and problems with acquiring land delayed construction until summer 1868, but once started, the navvies worked at a furious pace. The whole route was completed in just 16 months and opened for goods traffic on 1 September 1869. The finished line rose 232 ft in 2¾ miles and involved some substantial engineering, especially around Graig Fawr and Graig Bach where the permanent way was laid on a shelf blasted out of solid rock. There were also some stiff gradients, notably a long run at 1 in 45 north of Meliden where the lack of grip in wet weather became a curse for the crews of southbound trains.

The next major development was the introduction of a passenger service, which locals first campaigned for in 1895–6. At this time, the LNWR declined on the grounds that existing locomotives and rolling stock were too expensive for the probable traffic, but when a second petition reached

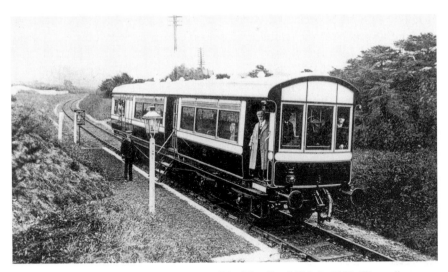

A fine picture of LNWR Railmotor No. 1 at Rhuddlan Road Halt in 1905. The rudimentary station facilities were augmented in later years by a shed at the south end of the platform, but they never amounted to very much and it is hardly surprising that they have vanished without trace. The halt was situated at GR 066821, just north of St Melyd Golf Links

Clwyd Record Office, Hawarden

Euston in May 1905 it was rapidly approved. The difference this time was that the company now had three railmotors under construction at Crewe and Wolverton Works – a pioneering attempt to provide low cost transport for lightly used routes. The railmotors were essentially a powered coach with a small steam engine enclosed at one end; in effect, a steam-powered precursor of the modern diesel railbus. The Dyserth branch was chosen as the line on which they would be tested and they duly began operations on 28 August 1905. Rail level platforms (actually a bed of cinders encased in a timber frame) were installed at Rhuddlan Road, Meliden and Dyserth, followed by others at Chapel Street, Prestatyn (1906), St Melyd Golf Links (1923) and Allt-y-Graig (1928).

At this point in the narrative, it is necessary to turn back the clock to April 1880, when the LNWR drew up plans for an extension from Dyserth to Newmarket (modern Trelawnyd). Disappointed at the company's failure to implement these, a local landowner, Mr H.D. Pochin, built the first part of the route from Dyserth to Marian Mill himself. The idea was to stimulate the company into finishing the work, but Euston remained unmoved. However, the introduction of the Prestatyn–Dyserth passenger service breathed life back into the project, and in November 1905, the LNWR deposited plans for the Dyserth & Newmarket Light Railway which would utilize Pochin's earthworks and continue eastwards to Newmarket.

Unfortunately, the local authorities objected to a proposed level crossing south of Dyserth station and did not finally withdraw their objections until 1913. The following year, the nation's railways were placed under government control for the duration of World War I, and after 1918, improvements in vehicle technology gave road transport the edge. Discussions about the new line continued for another 3 years or more, but there was now little chance of it being built and the scheme fizzled out. Despite this, Pochin's trackbed – unused from first to last – survives to this day.

It is just as well that the LNWR did not extend the branch to Newmarket, for by the 1920s road competition was having a severe effect on the Dyserth passenger service. In 1905–6, the 48-seater railmotor had carried 30,000 passengers – a level of patronage so high that, at times, the timetable had to be abandoned and the train run up and down the branch as many times as possible. Twenty years later, however, the number of passengers on some trains did not even reach double figures. The LMS, into which the LNWR had been 'grouped' in 1923, ran at least 14 passenger trains daily until the end, but they were clearly making a substantial loss and were accordingly withdrawn on 20 September 1930. The replacement of the railmotors by loco-hauled push-and-pull units in 1922 no doubt exacerbated the service's poor economics. The only passenger trains after this date were occasional enthusiasts' specials, such as those which ran on 2 October 1955 and 22 March 1969.

The branch now resumed its original role as a freight-only line, until further erosion of its business by road competition forced the withdrawal of all goods services on 4 May 1964. The only traffic then remaining came from a substantial quarry at Dyserth, which had received its rail connection in November 1884. This supplied the line with a steady flow of crushed limestone and baked lime until 7 September 1973, when it too switched to road transport. The last train comprised two wagons of lime and one of limestone ballast – not an impressive load with which to end over a century of service.

The Lines Today

Although most of the Holywell Town branch closed in 1954, it took a quarter of a century for it to be found a new purpose. For many years it was used as an unofficial footpath by local schoolchildren, but in 1977 the formation of 'The Friends of Greenfield Valley' demonstrated to Delyn Borough Council that there was sufficient interest and support locally to justify turning the line into part of a heritage park. The council duly purchased the line in 1979 and restoration work was carried out by a contractor over the next five years. The route is now maintained by a volunteer scheme, which has proved very successful and effective thanks to the commitment of the volunteer workers.

The closure of the Dyserth branch was a long and drawn out affair. After 1973, the line remained in place in anticipation of merry-go-round trains which never materialized. Track relaying was scheduled for 1975 but was never carried out, although the siding at Dyserth which had provided the line's latter day traffic was lifted in that year. The rest of the track remained in place until spring 1980, when it was dismantled over a period of three months. The branch was finally declared non-operational on 24 June 1981, despite having been utterly rail-less for the previous twelve months.

By this time, the North Clwyd Railway Association had been formed with the aim of reopening the branch as a standard gauge tourist line. It proposed to do this in two stages (Meliden–Dyserth followed by Prestatyn–Meliden) and made a strong enough case to Rhuddlan Borough Council for the local authority to purchase the trackbed from BR in 1983. Unfortunately, the preservation scheme then foundered, leaving the council with an unused asset. The problem was resolved in 1990 when work began on converting the line into the Prestatyn–Dyserth Walkway, which opened to the public two years later. Financial assistance for this work was provided by the Welsh Development Agency and UK2000 Cymru, while the British Trust for Conservation Volunteers helped with treeplanting and repairs to masonry.

Walk 1 – Greenfield to Holywell (1¼ miles)

The most notable thing about this line, as mentioned in the introduction, is its gradient – 1 in 27 all the way, making it the steepest line over which the LNWR regularly worked passenger trains. Even the station platform at Holywell Town was on a gradient of 1 in 51. The branch started at Holywell Junction (GR 196779), where the station still survives – an elaborate building with castellations and two small towers that stood at either end of the canopy. Closed by BR on 14 February 1966, it became the first station in Wales to be scheduled for preservation, although one would scarcely believe it nowadays: an application of black paint and neglect by its owners have not done the building any favours.

After leaving the station in an easterly direction, the branch curved south and ran over a viaduct whose arches still accommodate a number of small businesses; it then crossed the A548 by a towering bridge, which acts as a convenient landmark for the free car park at GR 197774. This is where the

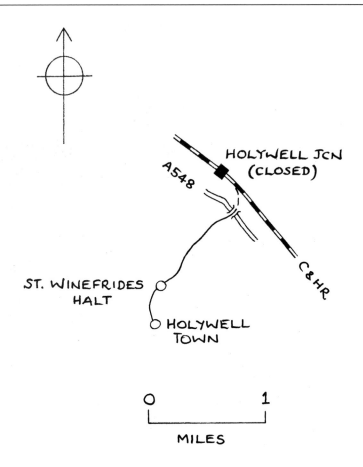

The Holywell Town Branch

trail proper starts, for the first quarter of a mile is privately owned and inaccessible. A path at the corner of the car park leads up on to the trackbed, and a quick diversion to the left will take you on to the bridge that you have just viewed from the road below. Unfortunately, this is something of a fool's errand, as I discovered, for the parapets are so high that only the world's tallest man can see over. The bridge supports a large variety of plant life, including some vigorous young trees, which the highway authority might be wise to remove.

Turning around, the line passes the ruins of Basingwerk Abbey on the right before entering a tunnel of deciduous trees which it follows all the way

This massive bridge over the A548 at Greenfield once carried trains between Holywell Junction and Holywell Town. Its vast proportions are made evident by the diminutive size of the approaching car

Author

to the site of Holywell Town station. Shortly after the abbey, it crosses an animal underpass at GR 195774 where a new steel bridge has been installed atop the original abutments. As the line continues, it occupies a ledge cut into the hillside with a stone retaining wall on the left, obviously installed to reinforce the cutting. It soon becomes apparent that the old trackbed has been well integrated with local footpaths, but the wooden signposts are an unfortunate target for the depredations of vandals.

At GR 193772, the trail passes the first of five reservoirs which were built in the eighteenth century to supply water to no less than eighteen separate water wheels that once existed between Holywell and Greenfield. Each of these produced approximately 65 horse power, an astonishing figure for such an early date. This is all part of the modern Greenfield Valley Heritage Park, which includes *inter alia* an historic farm with a sixteenth-century longhouse and a seventeenth-century barn. Shortly after the reservoirs, the line reaches a fork where you should bear left. This is the point where the LNWR branch diverges from the earlier Holywell Railway; if you turn right here, you will end up on the nearby B5121. St Winefride's Halt was situated nearby at GR 187766, but no trace of it remains today other than a sign erected by the local authority. The halt was built for visitors to the famous well, but in true railway fashion, they were given a long uphill walk!

The line continues to climb, curving to the left with more retaining walls evident until the site of Holywell Town station is reached at GR 187760. The terminus is heralded by an attractive double-arched stone bridge, which carries a minor road over the trail and now forms the centrepiece of a small local park. The station facilities, such as they were, were situated to the right on the far side of the bridge but they have been buried by modern landscaping; if you care to dig, the platform is still there! The excavated hollow in which the station once stood can only be seen now in old photographs, but a few lengths of spiked railway fencing survive here and there to give some clue as to the site's history. Being some distance below the road, the station was equipped with a unique tower lift worked by vacuum or steam power from the locomotive, which raised passengers' luggage up to road level.

Holywell town centre lies a short distance away and has a wide range of facilities; to reach it, simply proceed uphill bearing right. It is worth a visit as the buildings are elegant and well proportioned, and the place as a whole gives the impression that it has been well respected by modern developers and planners.

Walk 2 – Prestatyn to Dyserth (2¾ miles)

This is another short but interesting line which, like the Holywell Town branch, is uphill all the way. Dyserth passenger trains originally started from a bay platform at the west end of Prestatyn station and, after running past the signal-box where they collected the single line token, they then had to reverse on to the branch proper. (The Chester & Holyhead Railway had a morbid fear of facing connections on the main line, which its successor seems to have inherited.)

Although the trackbed can be traced right up to the BR station, this is not an appropriate place to start the walk. Make for the nearby bus station (GR 064829) and follow the lane along its north side to the site of a level crossing at GR 063828: this is the start of the trail proper and one can now walk without interruption all the way to Dyserth. Immediately south of the level crossing, there was once a siding on the left to the local gas works but the trail bears right, starting uphill almost immediately and passing a new doctors' surgery on the left. This marks the site of Bryn Rhosyn level crossing where a number of runaway freight trains, sliding down the grade in wet weather, reduced the gates to matchwood. The line continues under a 1930s-style concrete bridge, past a string of residential back gardens and then slips beneath the A547 Prestatyn–Abergele road before breaking out

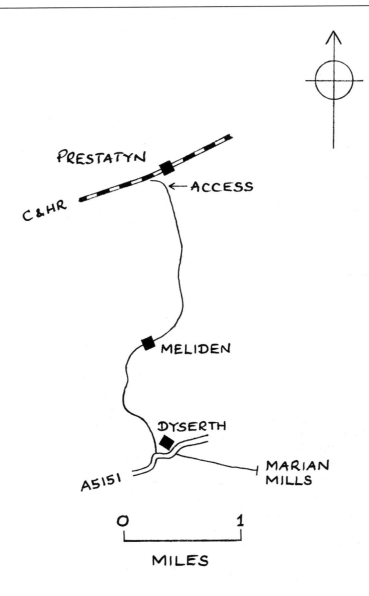

The Dyserth Branch

into the open near St Melyd Golf Links (GR 066818). The golf course actually straddles the line and one can see golfers and their caddies crossing the line in the distance. A nearby sign in the undergrowth warns readers to ring Wrexham 494 if the jib height of their crane risks snagging overhead wires – some chance!

By now, the trail offers impressive views of local hills, cliffs and mountains. It then curves west before reaching the site of Meliden station (GR 187766), where a stone goods shed survives together with a loading gauge which – to judge by the ropes dangling from it – has been used to improvise a pair of children's swings. The shed was occupied for a time by a vehicle repair firm and has recently been used by a company of undertakers, but is now in poor condition due to vandalism. This is a pity as it is a substantial and well-crafted building, which would present a totally different picture if carefully restored. Meliden once had a small yard that was kept busy with traffic from nearby quarries and lead mines, but that is all now long gone.

The section from Meliden to Dyserth is the most dramatic and heavily engineered of the whole line. The constant climb continues, passing a series

Meliden station on the former Dyserth branch, although somewhat run down, still retains something of the branch line atmosphere. This was once an important station for mineral traffic, much of it from Talargoch Lead Mines and a local limestone quarry. The loading gauge is an unusual survivor

Author

of man-made cliffs that were created when the navvies blasted their way through the rocky outcrops around Graig Fawr and Graig Bach. The cutting sides are all blackened, like the undersides of the bridges, but I suspect that this is explained more by geology than the exhaust of passing trains. The cuttings continue until shortly before Dyserth station, where an area of attractive woodland is entered; this lies beneath the ruins of Dyserth Castle, which was itself further ruined when the Victorians decided to use the site for limestone extraction – there were no planning regulations then. Immediately before the terminus, the line passes under bridges 7 and 8, the latter being a particularly elegant triple-arched structure. For the last 200 yd or so, old posts which once carried signal wires can be seen on the right, now rusted dark brown and completely incomprehensible to all but railway *cognoscenti*.

Beyond bridge 8, lines fanned out in two directions: the 'main' line curved left towards the goods facilities and primitive passenger station, while 'Lords Siding' bore right towards Dyserth Quarry. Walkers should follow the latter to the nearby A5151, noting bridge 9 *en route* which carries the track over a mountain stream. The road is reached at GR 063793: turn right here and proceed uphill for Dyserth village, or turn left to view the station which is

Bridge No. 8 north of Dyserth station is the finest on the branch. Immediately beyond, the track forked with the main branch bearing left into the station area, and Lord's Siding bearing right to reach Dyserth Quarry. This provided a steady flow of rail-borne limestone traffic until September 1973

Author

situated a short distance to the east at GR 064793. The property is in commercial use and has been fenced off, but the goods shed and Vale of Clwyd Farmers warehouse are still instantly recognizable from old photographs. The start of Mr Pochin's ill-fated extension to Newmarket lies on the opposite side of the road.

Further Explorations

It is a sad fact that, despite their scenic delights, only a very small proportion of Clwyd's abandoned railways have found reuse as recreational trails. The empty trackbed to Marian Mill is an obvious exception, but it is only three-quarters of a mile long.

Surprisingly, some traces of the original Holywell Railway still remain. When the LNWR built its branch to Holywell in 1912, it used the course of its predecessor between Greenfield and St Winefride's Halt, but then turned sharply east to reach the new terminus. South of St Winefride's, the original line curved to the west, passing below St Winefride's Well before reaching the Grange Cavern where limestone was extracted. Parts of this trackbed can still be traced, provided you know where to go and what to look for. Fortunately, the local Heritage Park has an expert guide in the form of Derek Richardson, some of whose guided walks incorporate this route.

West of Rhyl but still in the same general area, a minor line south of Kinmel Bay offers a short walk over the coastal plain. This is the Kinmel Camp Railway, a 4 mile branch opened in 1915 to serve an army camp west of Bodelwyddan church. After World War I, it was used by a local quarry company until it was closed in 1964. According to Clwyd County Council, there is an unsurfaced right of way along the trackbed from Towyn to the A547, and the authority's countryside service indicates that there is now an extension to the A55 making the whole route about 3 miles long. For some reason, detours have been created around two of the curves on the line but the trackbed can still be traced fairly easily. The start at the Towyn end is at GR 990794, where the walk initially heads west. At GR 983792, turn south, proceed as far as the A547 at GR 990776. On reaching the A547, follow the road west as far as GR 987776 and there turn south again. The trail finishes just north of the A55 at the site of a former level-crossing at GR 983762. The trackbed is clearly shown on the relevant OS Pathfinder sheet, but most of it has been removed from Landranger sheet 116 for some time. When even your map can't help you, you really do feel that you are exploring the back of beyond!

Transport and Facilities

Maps: Ordnance Survey: Landranger Series Sheet 116

Buses: Crosville Wales,
Ffynnon Groew Road, Rhyl, Clwyd, LL18 1WB
Telephone: Rhyl (0745) 343721

Clwyd County Council, Highways & Transportation,
Shire Hall, Mold, Clwyd, CH7 6NF
Telephone: Mold (0352) 752121 (direct line)

Trains: British Rail Telephone Enquiry Bureaux
Telephone: Chester (0244) 312624
or: Llandudno Junction (0492) 585151

If you don't want to walk both ways, the Crosville bus services along these trails are very convenient. The main routes are as follows:

A9   Holywell–Greenfield–Flint–Shotton–Chester
One bus per hour from 7.05 a.m. until 5.05 p.m.

A20   Holywell–Greenfield–Flint–Shotton Steelworks
Four journeys Mon-Fri, three on Sat. The last bus leaves
Holywell at 6.15 p.m.

35/36   Rhyl–Prestatyn–Dyserth–Rhyl Circular
An interesting route, worked by buses running both clockwise
and anticlockwise. There is a bus every half hour until
6.00 p.m., with journeys thereafter hourly *in alternate
directions* until 11.00 p.m.

All of these routes operate on Mondays to Saturdays only, with no service on Sundays. If you want to obtain up-to-date timetables, contact Clwyd County Council which publishes an excellent series of free timetable leaflets, available from Shire Hall (see above). The nearest railway stations are Flint, which is approximately 4 miles from Greenfield, and Prestatyn, which is a few minutes walk from the start of the trail to Dyserth. Both stations are on the Chester–Holyhead line.

    If the gradients on these walks work up a thirst, there are plenty of pubs to choose from in Holywell and Prestatyn, with others in Greenfield,

Meliden and Dyserth. The Royal Oak (on the B5121 near St Winefride's Halt) is recommended not only for its real ales, but also its proximity to the course of the Holywell Railway. As for the beers on offer, the big national brewers (anxious to get their share of the North Wales tourist trade) are well represented, although Banks, Burtonwood and Marstons ales can also be found. There are plenty of shops and eating places in Holywell and Prestatyn, but rather fewer in Dyserth – as might be expected, given that it is just a village.

2
LÔN EIFION

Caernarfon to Bryncir

Introduction

The LNWR's cross-country line from Caernarfon to Afon Wen offered almost 19 miles of steep gradients and imposing mountain scenery. For much of its life a quiet but well used local byway, it was transformed from 1947 – on summer Saturdays at least – by the opening of a Butlin's holiday camp at Penychain near Pwllheli, which led to the introduction of double-headed 10-coach holiday expresses. Due to the unusual use of the trackbed after closure (see *The Line Today*), the route is ideal for cycling and, struggling up the grade, one can well appreciate why two engines were needed to shift a 300 ton train full of holidaymakers and their luggage.

The local scenery is among the finest in Wales, and this is nowhere more obvious than along the course of the disused Welsh Highland Railway which connected with the Afon Wen line at Dinas Junction. This narrow gauge line has a history of extraordinary complexity which has continued to the present day; although the company went into liquidation in 1944, its trackbed remains in the hands of the Official Receiver and there are currently two rival schemes to reopen it – the railway preservationists' *coup* of the century if either one of them succeeds. In the meantime, a section of trackbed south of Beddgelert is open as an official footpath, and a walk along it is recommended if you want to get into the mountains that you have viewed at a distance from the former standard gauge line. Add to this the fact that there are no less than four operational narrow gauge steam lines nearby and you have an area of outstanding transport interest.

History

The first railway in Carnarvonshire was the Nantlle Railway, whose Act of 20 May 1825 authorized a tramway some 9 miles in length from copper mines and slate quarries in the Vale of Nantlle to quays below the walls of Caernarfon Castle. The line was built to the unusual gauge of 3 ft 6 in and opened for traffic in 1828; it ran due west from Nantlle to Penygroes before turning north for Caernarfon, along a course that was later used by the standard gauge Carnarvonshire Railway. A horse-drawn omnibus provided a connecting road service from Penygroes to Porthmadog, anticipating later railway developments by some thirty years.

In 1857, Edward Preston, then lessee of the Nantlle Railway, sought support for a Carnarvonshire Railway which would build a standard gauge line from Caernarfon to Porthmadog, using part of the old Nantlle formation. Although ultimately successful, this project had a very long incubation period due partly to Preston's close relations with the LNWR and its satellite, the Chester & Holyhead Railway. (No doubt locals remembered the ill-fated North Wales Railway, which collapsed in 1849 when it was discovered that the deputy chairman had loaned funds illegally to another railway with which he was involved.) Over the next five years, plans and counter-plans for lines south of Caernarfon were played out both locally and in Parliament, but on 29 July 1862, the Carnarvonshire Railway finally obtained its Act. It won through because it was the project with the most support locally, but its promoters were now Thomas Savin, the famous railway contractor, and Benjamin Piercy – who, ironically, had earlier signed an agreement with other parties not to trespass towards Caernarfon. This goes to show how much agreements were worth in the hotbed of Victorian railway politics!

Construction work started in early 1865, delayed by Savin's other commitments, but relatively little had to be built from scratch. It was discovered that the section from Afon Wen to Porthmadog was included in the Acts of both the Carnarvonshire company and the Aberystwith & Welch Coast Railway (sic), so by an agreement dated 13 December 1865 the CR astutely let its neighbour build the coastal section. Between Penygroes and Caernarfon, Savin speeded construction by abandoning the authorized route and re-building the Nantlle Railway as a standard gauge line, so all that remained was the 12 mile section from Penygroes to Afon Wen. By February 1866, this was complete together with the reconstruction of the Nantlle Railway from Penygroes to the River Seiont, south of Caernarfon.

It was lucky that the young company achieved so much so soon, for two disasters now struck in quick succession: the first was the collapse of its

While this view of Dinas Junction shows few of the station buildings, it does have the virtue of illustrating some narrow gauge coaches on the Welsh Highland Railway; these may be seen on the left behind the huge station signboard. The last WHR passenger train ran on 26 September 1936, and the paucity of passengers in this picture suggests why the service failed. The stationmaster's house behind the first coach provides a link with the present

Mike Hitches

bankers, Overend & Gurney, and the second was the bankruptcy of its contractor, Thomas Savin. The tangled web of events that followed need not concern us here, but the fact that the company's line had to be inspected thrice before opening reveals the quiet desperation with which it sought to obtain revenue. Its line from Caernarfon to Afon Wen finally opened on 2 September 1867, with trains continuing over the Cambrian (formerly A&WCR) line to Porthmadog and Penrhyndeudraeth until 10 October that year.

The arrangements at the Caernarfon end of the line were somewhat inconvenient, for the CR terminus at Pant (GR 482615) was situated some 1½ miles south of the Bangor & Carnarvon Railway's earlier terminus on the north-western edge of the town (GR 482632). To make matters worse, when the Carnarvon & Llanberis Railway opened on 1 August 1869, it used a third station at Morfa situated midway between the other two! This awkward situation was resolved on 5 July 1870, when the CR and C&LR opened a cross-town link which tunnelled beneath Castle Square to reach the B&C station, where all services were henceforth concentrated; the stations at Pant and Morfa were closed on 1 August the same year.

Bryncir was typical of the minor halts on the Afon Wen line with its diminutive buildings and neatly tended flower beds. The station was well sited in the village, which lies a few yards out of frame on the left, but the railway made more money from livestock travelling to and from the adjoining cattle market than the local human population. Little remains of this scene today other than the overgrown trackbed and a length of the Up platform on the right

Mike Hitches

By now the LNWR had got its hooks into the Carnarvonshire Railway, as was made evident in March 1869 when three of its directors resigned, transferring their shares to LNWR counterparts. The inevitable Act followed in 1870 whereby the LNWR acquired the local company for the sum of £234,260 10s 9d, but the takeover did at least eliminate any residual money problems: the early years of Euston's rule were characterized by a series of improvements, not least of which was the regauging of the rest of the Nantlle Railway bar the quarry lines that radiated out from its new Nantlle terminus, built in December 1871. It is interesting to note that these quarry lines retained both the 3 ft 6 in gauge and horse power until final closure in 1963 (see below). Due to the Carnarvonshire Railway's takeover of the Nantlle in 1867, this ancient horse-drawn tramway passed to British Railways in 1948 and was the only part of the national network to use this unique gauge.

At opening, stations were provided at Pwllheli Road (subsequently renamed Llanwnda), Groeslon, Penygroes, Brynkir (*sic*), Chwilog and Afon Wen, which was the junction with the Cambrian Coast line. The latter was a desolate place, built purely for the convenience of the railways which used it; there was barely a house in sight and, had the station been built any further south, it would have been in the sea. Further stations were subsequently added at Dinas, Pant Glas, Ynys and Llangybi. I have been unable to determine the level of service at opening, but by 1904 there were seven weekday passenger trains in each direction, plus a host of freight workings. In subsequent years, the service was gradually improved: by 1922, there were nine passenger trains from Caernarfon to Afon Wen with eleven the other way, and by 1939 there were ten each way. Some of these ran through to destinations as diverse as Llandudno Junction, Liverpool Lime Street, Manchester Exchange and Euston, not to mention the many extra services that ran on summer Saturdays that year.

The line became part of the London, Midland & Scottish Railway in 1923 and passed to the London Midland Region of British Railways with nationalization in 1948. Falling patronage on the branches forced the LMS to introduce the first economies by withdrawing passenger services to Llanberis and Nantlle in 1930 and 1932 respectively but, despite this, the Llanberis line remained a popular destination for summer excursions. Many passengers on these trains transferred at Llanberis on to the Snowdon Mountain Railway – Britain's only rack and pinion line – which had opened in 1896. The LMS also lasted long enough to witness a substantial increase in business brought about in 1947 by the opening of Butlin's holiday camp at Penychain. This brought heavy tourist traffic on to the line with the result that the passing loops at Dinas, Bryncir and Llangybi had to be lengthened to accommodate ten-coach trains.

The summer 'Land Cruises' (see Chapter 3) that ran on Mondays to Fridays between 1951 and 1961 also kept the route busy, but unfortunately all of this traffic was seasonal. An article published in the *Railway Magazine* in September 1958 summarized the line's dilemma pithily: 'On Saturdays during the summer season, it changes from its usual role of a more or less somnolent branch to that of a busy main line'. Alas, by the 1960s British Railways had little use for somnolent branch lines (the widespread switch to road transport had seen to that) and the inevitable closures duly followed. The feeders to Nantlle and Llanberis closed to freight on 2 December 1963 and 3 September 1964 respectively. During 1964, stations on the 'main' line also closed to freight, Pant Glas already having lost such services in 1952. Finally, on 7 December 1964, passenger trains from Caernarfon to Afon Wen were withdrawn, thus bringing to an end nearly a century of continuous public service.

Locals were not particularly happy about the withdrawal (nor for that matter was Carnarvonshire County Council, which published its objections in March 1964) but the Minister of Transport, Ernest Marples, overruled them. On the plus side, he insisted that the link from Bangor to Caernarfon was retained, although this too was closed on 5 January 1970 – barely six months after the investiture of the Prince of Wales at Caernarfon Castle on 1 July 1969. However, four months later, the famous Britannia Bridge over

Menai Strait caught fire, isolating Anglesey and Holyhead from the rest of the rail network, and Caernarfon was hurriedly brought into use as an emergency terminal for the Irish traffic. This lasted until 5 February 1972, when the bridge was reopened and railways in Caernarfon disappeared for good. The town's only chance of a rail connection now lies in the revival of the Welsh Highland Railway (see below).

The Line Today

The rails between Caernarfon and Afon Wen were removed in 1968, after which Carnarvonshire County Council purchased the section from the River Seiont to Afon Wen. In 1974, the newly formed Gwynedd County Council – continuing the policy of its predecessor – purchased the section from the River Seiont to the south end of Vaynol Tunnel, near Bangor. In so doing, it assumed responsibility for all bridges, culverts, fences and retaining walls, but said that it might sell off any sections that proved surplus to requirements.

East of Caernarfon, a few 'awkward' bridges were demolished and the A487 road straightened out, but a lot of the trackbed remains unused to this day. On the Afon Wen line, it was initially thought that the section south of Llanwnda would be taken over by a brake manufacturing company that wanted a test track for its products, but it was acquired instead by McAlpine, the building contractors. In 1976, this company built a tarmac road along the formation from Llanwnda to Cefn Graianog (GR 463487), complete with passing places and Armco barriers, so that lorries carrying aggregate to the Dinorwig hydro-electric scheme could keep off the public highway. (Regrettably, McAlpine also demolished the surviving stations at Llanwnda and Penygroes.) The aggregate traffic ceased in 1983, after which the route reverted to local authority ownership.

By this time, the idea of creating a walk and cycle trail along the line had been mooted, and the existence of McAlpine's road provided a strong all-weather surface over a substantial length of it; all that remained was the installation of a decent surface over the 4 mile section from Caernarfon to Llanwnda. This followed in due course, but the 3½ miles from Graianog to Bryncir were left untouched as they are rather remote. The 'Cycle Route' legend that appears on the OS map is an exaggerated description of what actually exists here, for it amounts to no more than a grass-covered track that one shares with the local sheep. From Bryncir to Afon Wen, it appears that the local authority has carried out its threat to sell off anything that was surplus to requirements, for parts of the trackbed are clearly in private ownership, while others are totally overgrown.

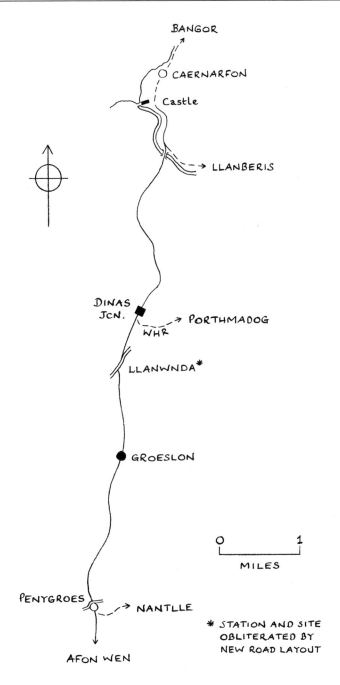

Lôn Eifion (North)

The Walk (12½ Miles)

This walk divides roughly in two: the section from Caernarfon to Penygroes is largely enclosed and tree-lined, while that from Penygroes to Bryncir is generally open with superb views of the surrounding mountains and Caernarfon and Cardigan bays. The whole route is waymarked as a cycle trail and, while open to walkers as well, a bike does have the advantage of avoiding any tedium that might arise on the tarmacked section. Whatever mode of transport you use, the views south of Penygroes repay a visit handsomely.

The station at Caernarfon was situated at GR 482362 but the vast site now accommodates two car parks – proof, were it needed, of the victory locally of road over rail transport. At its peak, Caernarfon was the largest of all the branch line stations in North Wales and the sheer size of the place is still impressive: retaining walls survive around the edge of the site, while slabs from the platforms have been used to form the central reservations in each of the two car parks. Continuing in a south-westerly direction, the line threads its way past the backs of shops and offices, and is largely abandoned bar a few short lengths which have been used by local businesses as narrow car parks; most of the trackbed is grassed over and seems something of a wasted asset. Shortly before the castle, the line plunges into a 164 yd tunnel which emerges near the quayside, once the site of extensive sidings but now, predictably, yet another car park.

The official route starts from the south side of the tunnel at GR 480626. The formation at this point is rather wide and there were plans in the nineteenth century for a station here, but it would have been a very cramped affair when one considers the amount of space the railway occupied on the other side of the town. Hemmed in by a massive retaining wall on the left and quayside warehouses on the right, there was simply no room for expansion. There were originally three lines here: from left to right, the Llanberis branch, the Afon Wen branch and a headshunt for the quayside network. All of these were lifted long ago and the whole area has succumbed to the now familiar curse, but at least this is the last car park we shall see for some miles . . .

Continuing southwards, one passes under two distinctive footbridges which spring out from the retaining wall on the left before reaching a replica level crossing gate which marks the start of the trail proper. In a quarter of a mile (GR 482618), the Llanberis branch curves away to the left along the north bank of the Afon Seiont, while our line bears right and crosses the river by a magnificent double-span bridge. If you have time, make your way down to the water's edge to get a good look at this structure (there are steps

Tourists who park on Caernarfon Quay may be forgiven for not appreciating that it was once a labyrinth of railway sidings, complete with wagon turntables. Caernarfon Castle dominates the scene, no longer disturbed by trains rumbling through the tunnel that burrowed under Castle Square

Author

at the north end of the eastern parapet); it might not seem much from the trackbed, but you'll think differently when you view it from below. Just south of the river, the line passes under a road bridge (GR 482616) beyond which it joins the course of the old Nantlle Railway; according to the September 1958 issue of the *Railway Magazine*, this bridge includes a separate span for the tramway at the north-west corner, although vegetation has probably rendered it invisible. (I only discovered this after I had visited the area.) The original Pant station was situated a few yards to the south on top of the cutting on the left-hand side at about GR 482615.

Continuing south the going is easy, punctuated by the remains of several brick-built gangers' huts which are a feature of the line throughout. Near Bontnewydd, the trail crosses the Afon Gwyrfai by another substantial bridge (GR 479600), east of which lies one of the few tangible reminders of the Nantlle Railway – a tramway bridge over the same river (GR 480599). The next major feature is Dinas Junction, where Gwynedd County Council has established a depot. This occupies the whole of the station site and the cycle trail has been diverted to the very edge of the formation on the west. Dinas was given the appendage 'Junction' on account of its being the

This viaduct over the Afon Seiont is situated at GR 482618, about ¾ mile south of Caenarfon Castle. It is very unprepossessing from the trackbed and is easily missed, but the view from the water's edge reveals its true scale

Author

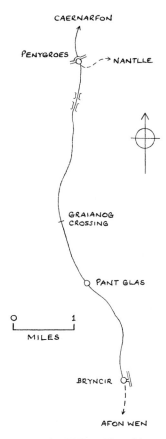

Lôn Eifion (South)

interchange station with the narrow gauge Welsh Highland Railway; several buildings of WHR origin can be seen inside the compound, including the large transhipment shed, while the trackbed itself is used to enable GCC vehicles to get from one part of the site to another. Elsewhere in the village, the trackbed survives intact although it is impenetrably overgrown; it may be viewed from a road-over-rail bridge on the nearby A487 at GR 477584.

Back on the line to Afon Wen, the trail continues for another half mile to the A499 at Llanwnda, where the station has been demolished; it used to stand at GR 473577. (The white road shown on the OS map between Dinas and Llanwnda is, in fact, incorrect; the trackbed is just a loose trail finished in rolled limestone dust.) South of the A499, however, the trackbed is McAlpine's former haul road and a very convenient cycle trail it makes too. The route now climbs steadily to Groeslon, where the station site accommodates a small car park for trail users. There was a level crossing and passing loop here; traces of the two platforms can still be found (one was lower than the other), but the single-storey station building and timber passenger shelters have all been demolished. The nearby pub, the Llanfair Arms, is of some interest, for its sign tells how it was previously known as the 'Onion Head' after the physical appearance of its landlord – a Welsh colloquialism which clearly predates political correctness!

Penygroes, the next station (GR 467530), is preceded by a long embankment which gives some idea of the visual splendours to follow. Penygroes was, and still is, the largest settlement on the line south of Caernarfon. It once boasted a substantial brick-built station complete with passing loop, signal-box, small goods yard and bay platform for the Nantlle branch. At its height, it employed a staff of seven, many of whom must have been involved with the slate traffic that came from the quarries east of Nantlle. The whole area has a rather bleak and lifeless look now that all this

The Welsh Highland Railway may have been closed for over half a century, but much of its permanent way and many of its engineering features still remain. This girder bridge south of Beddgelert carries the trackbed, now a public footpath, across the Afon Glaslyn. Aberglaslyn Pass lies beyond, where geographical constraints forced the railway builders to bore a series of tunnels and cut a ledge into the mountainside. Only 3½ miles of the line can be walked officially, but this is one of the most scenic railway walks anywhere in the United Kingdom – don't miss it!

Author

has been demolished. Some decorative stonework has been installed on the east side of the site and the county council has deposited a bizarre Italianate shelter on the Up platform, but being built from timber, the local vandals have had their way with it. It will be reduced to a wooden skeleton unless some remedial work is carried out soon.

South of Penygroes, the gradient stiffens as the line traverses a pair of viaducts separated by a high embankment; from the top of the viaduct at GR 466520, the Afon Llynfi can be heard below cascading over rocks on its seaward course to Pontllynfi. The gradient remains steep as the line skirts around Mynydd Graig Goch, with the countryside ahead becoming wilder all the time. McAlpine's haul road comes to an abrupt end at GR 463487; the fact that the OS map shows it continuing all the way to Bryncir is just wishful thinking! The next feature is the site of Pant Glas station, which is met at GR 469472 between an abandoned level crossing and a bridge over a stream. This remote halt, serving a tiny and equally remote settlement, was added some three years after the line opened. It had a single platform with a single-storey stone building, a token siding and a station-master's house. Traffic was light at all times and it is remarkable that it continued to serve passengers until January 1957 (freight facilities were withdrawn two years earlier). The station-master's house is still intact but the timber-faced platform is buried beneath deep vegetation.

Beyond Pant Glas, the line draws close to the A487 and both routes run more or less parallel for the last two miles to Bryncir. The trail here suffers from a little surface water after rain, but this should not pose a problem outside the winter months. The rustic image is reinforced by sheep and horses grazing the line: the sheep scurry away as you approach, bleating in panic, but the horses hold their ground. This can be a problem, as I discovered, if a horse has taken post on the far side of a gate that opens outwards – how do you persuade half a ton of horse to stand aside? On the engineering side, there are two small bridges over streams, plus a number of truncated signals, cut off about 6 in above the ground.

The approach to Bryncir is heralded by a slurry lagoon to the west of the trail and then, suddenly, one alights at the site of the village station (GR 479447). How things have changed here. Bryncir was once a passing place with two platforms, a small goods yard and cattle dock, but the station buildings have been razed to the ground and the platforms are barely discernible among the encroaching vegetation. It used to be a busy place – especially on summer Saturdays – and there was a good livestock trade from the nearby cattle market, which today provides one of the few tangible links with the past. Given the small size of Bryncir village, one wonders how it came to acquire a railway station in the first place, but the answer lies in the poor state of nineteenth-century roads.

At the end of another busy day, *Gelert* puffs quietly out of Porthmadog station back to the shed at Gelerts Farm Works on the revived Welsh Highland Railway. The peaks of Snowdon rise enticingly in the background; perhaps one day Welsh Highland trains will run through the mountains again

Author

The line to Afon Wen is securely fenced off, so walkers and cyclists must now use the old station approach road to reach the nearby A487. About a quarter of a mile to the south, there is a garden centre, petrol station and village shop, but the local pub – the Bryncir Arms – was boarded up when I visited. There is a bus stop nearby, which is well served by buses to Caernarfon.

Further Explorations

There are two other railway walks within easy reach of Caernarfon: the first is the Bangor–Glasinfryn route, which is described briefly in Appendix B, and the second is the Welsh Highland Railway south of Beddgelert. The Welsh Highland route is highly recommended. As noted earlier, the history of this company is extremely complex and out of all proportion to its success or influence. In essence, the engineering difficulties of the route and the meagre traffic from local quarries led to a succession of small local companies trying their luck – and failing.

The WHR was formed on 30 March 1922 by the merger of two earlier companies, the North Wales Narrow Gauge Railway and the Porthmadog, Beddgelert & South Snowdon Railway. While ultimately unsuccessful like its predecessors, it did succeed in creating a continuous route from Dinas to Porthmadog by constructing the missing link from Beddgelert to Croesor Junction. The predictable financial problems forced closure to all traffic on 31 December 1931, but on 9 July 1934, the Festiniog Railway leased the line and ran tourist trains during the summers of 1934, 1935 and 1936. However, not even the Festiniog could make a profit on it and the last passenger train duly ran on 26 September 1936. Freight services were withdrawn on 1 June the following year.

During World War II, the track was requisitioned to help with the war effort and removed between 1941 and 1942. The company was wound up on 7 February 1944, but the trackbed remained in the hands of the Official Receiver – a happy accident which accounts for the fact that most of it has survived intact, complete with many engineering works, for over fifty years. In 1964 a new company, the Welsh Highland Light Railway (1964) Ltd, was formed to rebuild the line but has since clashed with the Ffestiniog Railway which, having completed its own reopening to Blaenau in 1982, now sees the Welsh Highland as a natural outlet for expansion. Both the 1964 company and the Ffestiniog want to reinstate the whole of the line to Dinas and extend it northwards to Caernarfon via the LNWR, but it seems that Gwynedd County Council favours the former. While the protagonists slog it out, walkers are free to enjoy a fascinating ramble along the trackbed from Beddgelert to Ynys Fer-las.

The route may be joined at GR 590473, about half a mile south of Beddgelert on the A498. The first 2 miles are the most popular and are extremely well used, especially on sunny afternoons during the summer. The line offers an amazing wealth of engineering features, including a variety of bridges (of both stone and girder construction) and no less than three tunnels, as it claws its way through the narrow Aberglaslyn Pass. Families are much in evidence here: children enjoy splashing about in the Afon Glaslyn and relish the excitement of exploring the tunnels, where they make appropriate sound effects at high volume. They probably don't even notice the magnificent scenery, or the variety of mosses and lichens that have colonized the stone walls of the cuttings! While in Beddgelert, it is also worth looking out for a bridge over the A498 at GR 588478; although this was never used, it was built as part of a projected electric railway that was intended to reach Porthmadog via a route that involved lesser gradients. Unused abutments either side of the Afon Glaslyn stand a few hundred yards to the east, mute reminders of another railway promoter's abandoned dream.

If after all this railway rambling you want to 'let the train take the strain', there is no shortage of opportunities: you can choose from the Llanberis Lake Railway, the Snowdon Mountain Railway, the Ffestiniog Railway and the nascent Welsh Highland Railway. The termini for the first two are situated within a few hundred yards of each other in Llanberis, while the termini for the others are about half a mile apart in Porthmadog. A walk along the trackbed south of Beddgelert made quite an impression on me, so I plumped for the Welsh Highland and was pleased to discover that my train would be hauled by *Russell*, one of the original WHR locomotives. Perhaps in time it will have more than half a mile of track to run on.

Finally, there may soon be a preserved standard gauge railway in the vicinity. Traffic on the Anglesey line from Gaerwen Junction to Amlwch ceased in September 1993 and the line has since been mothballed pending sale to the Isle of Anglesey Railway Company. If this bid fails, it would make a wonderful cycle trail!

Transport and Facilities

Maps: Ordnance Survey: Landranger Series Sheets 115 and 123

Buses: Express Motors, Gerallt, Bontnewydd,
            Caernarfon, Gwynedd, LL54 7UN
            Telephone: Caernarfon (0286) 674570

Crosville Wales, Beach Road,
Bangor, Gwynedd, LL57 1AB
Telephone: Bangor (0248) 370295

Gwynedd County Council,
Economic Development & Planning Department,
County Offices, Caernarfon, Gwynedd, LL55 1SH
Telephone: Caernarfon (0286) 679535 (direct line)

Trains: British Rail Telephone Enquiry Bureaux
Telephone: Holyhead (0407) 769222
        or: Llandudno Junction (0492) 585151

Cycle Hire: Beddgelert Bikes, Hafod Ruffydd Uchaf,
Beddgelert Forest, Beddgelert, Gwynedd, LL55 4UU
Telephone: Beddgelert (0766) 86434

While the trackbed of the Welsh Highland Railway is too
knobbly to cycle, a bike does offer a good way of exploring
this exceptionally scenic area, especially if you want to trace the
line from local roads. Beddgelert Bikes are open all the year
round, seven days a week, from 9.00 a.m. to 5.00 p.m. during
the winter and from 9.00 a.m. to dusk during the summer. Hire
charges start at £3.00.

When you first view the wild and empty terrain around Pant Glas and
Bryncir, you may despair of ever seeing a bus again, but fear not – the
service is remarkable, thanks to the proximity of the A487. There are three
services in all (numbered 1, 1c and 2) which collectively provide at least one
bus an hour between Bryncir and Caernarfon. The last of them leaves
Bryncir at about 11 p.m., but there are very few buses on a Sunday – four or
five during the summer, perhaps only one in the winter. If you wish to use
these, you would be well advised to obtain the comprehensive public
transport guide from Gwynedd County Council, which includes the
timetables for every bus and train service in the county. The Caernarfon
buses stop at Pant Glas, Nasareth, Penygroes, Groeslon, Llanwnda and
Bontnewydd, all of which are on or close to Lôn Eifion. Bus services to
Beddgelert run from Caernarfon and Porthmadog: there are approximately
six journeys on weekdays and four on summer Sundays, all running at 2-
hourly intervals.

As for refreshments, there are plenty of pubs in Caernarfon and
Penygroes, and one each in Bontnewydd, Dinas, Llanwnda and Groeslon.
(The Goat Hotel at Llanwnda used to overlook the railway station.) South

of Penygroes, the countryside is very remote and facilities are accordingly hard to come by, but the village shop in Bryncir can provide emergency rations in the form of pies, confectionery and soft drinks. In Beddgelert, the best bet is the Prince Llewelyn, which is probably the only pub in these islands to have been hit by a meteor; although a hotel, walkers are welcome. On the down side, many of the beers available in this area are national mass-produced products, although Burtonwood, Marstons and Robinsons do have a few outlets.

3
THE MAWDDACH ESTUARY

Barmouth to Dolgellau

Introduction

The Mawddach Estuary lies in a wide valley some 6½ miles long running from Llanelltyd near Dolgellau to just south of Barmouth. It is enclosed by mountains on all sides, that on the south being the famous Cadair Idris which rises to a height of 2,928 ft above sea level. The valley is glacial, although its true shape is hidden by over 150 ft of silt which have created the flat-bottomed form which the visitor sees today – the result of rising sea levels and gradually sinking land. The scenery is on a grand scale, and the estuary with its many tributaries forms a rich habitat for wildlife.

In the eighteenth century, the Mawddach was a busy shipping route: goods inward included coal from South Wales together with lime and manure for the farms, while goods outwards included slate from local quarries and coarse cloth from the weavers of Dolgellau. The number of creeks and widespread availability of native oak allowed shipbuilding to flourish, but the river's trade was stolen and the shipbuilding wiped out following the arrival of the Barmouth–Dolgellau railway. Now that too has gone, but what remains is a fine railway walk that offers the only way to see the estuary properly. According to the RSPB, which has a base locally at Penmaenpool, the spectacular scenery here usually makes a deep impression on visitors, and I know of few estuarial walks that can match the interest or splendour of this one.

History

The railway line between Barmouth and Dolgellau is often regarded as the western end of a 54 mile GWR branch from Ruabon, but this is a misleading view. For fifty-five of its ninety-odd years, it was actually a branch of the Cambrian Railways, and a Cambrian constituent – the Aberystwith & Welch Coast Railway (*sic*) – was responsible for building most of it. The A&WCR was incorporated by an Act dated 22 July 1861. It was authorized to construct a line along the Cambrian Coast, which, with hotels springing up between Aberystwyth and Barmouth, it saw as an area of growing but untapped tourist potential. It was responsible for the three lines which now radiate from Dovey Junction to Machynlleth, Aberystwyth and Pwllheli, while the Dolgellau branch was added later as a defensive move against the Great Western, which was advancing westwards from Ruabon down the Dee Valley.

The Act for the Dolgellau branch was passed on 29 July 1862, by which time work was already well advanced on the line to Aberystwyth. The company was obliged to construct this first in order to prevent the hostile Newtown & Machynlleth Railway from exercising its right to do so if the A&WCR failed to complete the line by 1 August 1864. The A&WCR did not hang about; trains began running from Machynlleth to Borth on 1 July 1863 and reached Aberystwyth just under a year later on 23 June 1864. With the threat to its empire removed, the company then turned to the

This undated photograph from the early 1960s shows a busy scene at Morfa Mawddach with BR standard class locomotives much in evidence. The workings, from left to right, are probably Machynlleth–Barmouth, Barmouth–Machynlleth and Dolgellau–Barmouth

Author's Collection

Pwllheli line which was opened in a truly piecemeal fashion. The section from Aberdovey Harbour to Llwyngwril opened on 24 October 1863, followed by an extension from Llwyngwril to Penmaenpool on 3 July 1865. This remained isolated from the rest of the company's network until 14 August 1867, when the link from Dovey Junction to Aberdovey was opened. North of the Afon Mawddach, trains began running between Afon Wen and Penrhyndeudraeth on 2 September 1867, but these were operated by the Carnarvonshire Railway working south from Caernarfon. The entire route was not completed until 10 October 1867, from which date trains could finally run all the way from Machynlleth to Pwllheli; but still the Dolgellau branch remained incomplete.

The main feature of the coast line was the half-mile bridge over the Afon Mawddach between Barmouth Junction (latterly Morfa Mawddach) and Barmouth Town, which remains to this day the longest viaduct in Wales. It opened to horse-drawn traffic on 3 June 1867, prior to which passengers were required to leave their train at Barmouth Ferry (on the site of modern Fairbourne station) and complete their journey to Barmouth by boat. At low tide, this involved walking over a 300 yd bar of rough gravel, which a contemporary commentator described quaintly as 'a mode of proceeding not very convenient for ladies and children'. Passengers must have been relieved when through steam services began using the bridge on 10 October, and even more pleased when a footpath over the bridge was authorized the following year.

While all this was going on, the Cambrian Railways had been formed on 25 July 1864 by an amalgamation of local companies controlling the route from Whitchurch to Machynlleth via Oswestry and Newtown; the A&WCR joined them on 5 July 1865, extending this network to Aberystwyth and Pwllheli. Meanwhile, the inexorable advance of the GWR from Ruabon to Barmouth continued apace via a series of small and nominally independent satellite companies, the last of which – the Bala and Dolgelly Railway (*sic*) – opened its line from Bala to Dolgellau on 4 August 1868. Frustrated by the 2 mile gap between Dolgellau and Penmaenpool, the B&DR and GWR obtained powers to complete the missing link if the Cambrian had not done so by August 1869. This did the trick. The line was built post-haste and, on 21 June 1869, Cambrian trains began running into Dolgellau where they terminated at a temporary wooden platform at the west end of the B&DR goods yard; they began running through to the permanent station on 1 August.

The arrangements at Dolgellau were somewhat extravagant but mercifully did not extend to two stations on separate sites as originally planned. The junction between the two railways was situated just west of the station and Cambrian trains had to traverse 28 chains of B&DR track to reach their terminus. Anyone who thought the finished station a little grand for a small

Dolgellau was unusual in being served by two separate stations built on the same site, an arrangement which led to the wholesale duplication of facilities. In this fine view from 1958, the stations face each other across the rails, while the rival companies' signal-boxes are framed by the footbridge. Note the clerestory camping coach in the distance, a reminder of the days when the railway could provide the accommodation for a cheap holiday as well as the means of getting there. The station site has now been flattened in connection with works for the modern Dolgellau bypass, although much of it survives as an open space used by Dolgellau Farmers. The base of the signal-box on the right still survives and provides a point of reference with this view from the past

David Ibbotson

market town would have been absolutely right, for it was in fact two entirely separate stations on opposite sides of the running lines. Only the mad politics of Victorian railway construction could produce a situation so wasteful and bizarre: the two companies had their own station buildings, signal-boxes and staffs, who kept themselves apart for fifty-five years. The GWR rationalized the situation after 1922, when the Cambrian came under its control as part of the grouping. (The GWR had absorbed the B&DR in 1877 and the other companies between Ruabon and Bala in 1896.)

By the 1870s, the line carried two Down and three Up trains between Ruabon and Barmouth, supplemented by a number of local workings such as Corwen to Barmouth. The most intensive service operated between the wars, when the tourist traffic necessitated six Ruabon–Barmouth workings daily on top of a much expanded local service. The Ruabon–Barmouth trains carried through coaches to Pwllheli from Birkenhead, Manchester,

Birmingham, Reading and Paddington, while local journeys to Barmouth included four from Dolgellau and two from Drws-y-Nant. After World War II, however, the line never fully recovered; Sunday trains were an early casualty and the remaining services were progressively simplified, especially after withdrawal of the connecting Denbigh–Corwen and Ffestiniog–Bala trains. Despite this, the line enjoyed something of an Indian summer between 1951 and 1961, when it played host to a series of popular 'Land Cruises' which ran variously between Monday and Friday during the summer season. The route of these trains is particularly interesting, for it includes many abandoned lines in North Wales: starting at Rhyl on the north coast, they ran to Denbigh, Corwen, Bala, Dolgellau and Barmouth, where a stop for lunch was made; they then continued back to Rhyl via Harlech, Afon Wen, Caernarfon, Bangor and Llandudno Junction.

The crunch finally came during the Beeching era. The Cambrian Coast line was then served – as it had been for many years – by no less than four separate connecting routes from the north and east. Beeching resolved that only one of these should be retained and the choice narrowed to Ruabon–Barmouth or Shrewsbury–Aberystwyth, the ex-Cambrian main line. Ruabon–Barmouth had the advantage of being the shortest route from north-west England, but the Cambrian main line was eventually retained because it served a larger population and, at Shrewsbury, had much better connections with the remaining rail network. The inevitable closures duly followed. Morfa Mawddach closed to goods traffic on 4 November 1963, followed by Arthog, Penmaenpool and Dolgellau on 14 December 1964. The withdrawal of passenger services between Ruabon and Morfa Mawddach was scheduled for 18 January 1965, but nature intervened on 12–13 December 1964 with a severe storm which breached the line east of Dolgellau. With closure imminent, repairs were clearly out of the question; the section from Llangollen to Dolgellau closed immediately, although local services were resumed between Ruabon and Llangollen, and Dolgellau and Barmouth. On Monday 18 January 1965, Crosville introduced a new D94 bus service from Barmouth to Wrexham and, with that, the Dolgellau branch – and the ex-GWR line to Ruabon – were finished.

The Cambrian Coast line, including Barmouth Bridge, hung on by its fingertips. The precariousness of its future became painfully apparent in 1970, when a Ministry of Transport cost-benefit study showed that 'even with economies, [retention of] the Machynlleth–Pwllheli line was difficult to justify'. In March 1971, closure notices were accordingly posted at stations along the line between Dovey Junction and Pwllheli. Stung by the loss of rail facilities elsewhere in the area, local people and councils alike reacted vigorously; their opposition was vindicated by a public inquiry in June which found that closure of the line would cause genuine hardship and reduce traffic on the remaining line to Aberystwyth, thereby threatening the future of that as well. The full measure of hardship was particularly evident either side of the Barmouth Bridge, where removal of the one mile rail link would necessitate a 13 mile detour via a toll bridge at Penmaenpool, or a 17 mile detour via the edge of Dolgellau. It took some time for the government mandarins to reach a decision, but in July 1974 the whole of the coast line from Dovey Junction to Pwllheli was reprieved unconditionally.

A further threat came in October 1980, when British Rail closed Barmouth Bridge indefinitely following the discovery that it had become dangerous due to attack by *teredo navalis*, the common ship worm, which had made mincemeat of its wooden piers. During the winter of 1980–1, BR replaced the minimum number of affected piles, reopening the bridge on 22 May 1981 – on which day, incidentally, it sold no less than 8,000 'Welcome Back to Barmouth Bridge' day rover tickets, offering unlimited travel between Shrewsbury, Abertystwyth and Pwllheli. (Good value fills trains, even in this day and age.) It then declared that it looked to other bodies to help finance the rest of the restoration work. The reaction of these 'other bodies' was resounding in its silence but, fortunately for the Cambrian Coast line, locals pressed BR into action. The prime movers were the Cambrian Coast Line Action Group (CCLAG) and the local authorities, whose reward was a £1.5 million Barmouth Bridge repair programme. This was followed in late 1984 by the unveiling of a £4.7 million modernization plan for the route, including new Sprinter trains, radio signalling and automatic level crossings. The radio signalling heralded the closure and demolition of some 30 signal-boxes, although Barmouth South survived because it was a listed structure. Most of these changes had been implemented and 'bedded in' by the end of 1989.

The Line Today

After the line from Morfa Mawddach to Ruabon closed, the rails were left in place while the government reviewed broad policy issues. This moratorium changed nothing, however, and the track was eventually lifted in 1968. Two years later, plans were put forward for a 28 mile narrow gauge railway from Bala to Morfa Mawddach, but this too proved abortive; it was left to the Bala Lake Railway to revive a section of the line alongside Bala Lake in August 1972.

In 1977, most of Dolgellau station and much of the adjoining trackbed were buried beneath a new town bypass (possibly just as well considering the damage vandals had inflicted on the site), but by this time the old Merioneth County Council had purchased the trackbed between

Penmaenpool and Morfa Mawddach. This opened as an official railway walk in 1979. Stewardship of the trail has since passed to the Snowdonia National Park Authority, which extended it eastwards from Penmaenpool to the A493 about a mile from Dolgellau.

A section of the line at Morfa Mawddach has been laid with fine shale waste and developed as a trail for the disabled, complete with easy wheelchair access, seats and handrails; there are even wheelchair passing places! This starts at GR 628141. On the rest of the trail, the surface is flat, hard and dry, but it is much rougher by comparison. A perennial problem is flooding, which affects the modern trail just as the railway before it. In 1938, stationmaster W.T. Edwards of Arthog saved his life by clinging to a ground frame lever while flood waters swirled all around him; he eventually managed to climb on to the roof of a shed before being rescued by boat. I am not suggesting that anyone should go walking in weather like this, but it does explain why parts of the surface may be hard going.

The Walk (9½ Miles)

Keen to get a good look at the famous Barmouth Bridge, I started my walk at the western end in Barmouth. The trail can be picked up on the edge of the town at GR 619156, where the footpath over the bridge leaves the A496 Barmouth–Dolgellau road. Before crossing the bridge proper, I came to a small toll booth where pedestrians make their modest contribution to its upkeep (30p return or £7 annual season ticket at 1992 prices). In order to simplify matters, the tolls are charged in one direction only.

At first sight, the bridge impresses by its sheer length rather than towering grandeur, but this is misleading for its foundations lie 120 ft below water level. The first section is of steel construction and includes two bow-string spans which rotate on a central pier; this was constructed between 1899 and 1909 to replace an earlier sliding mechanism, whereby one span rolled back on wheels atop another. This took two men 37 minutes to open and close and attracted much adverse comment from Captain Tyler, the Railway Inspector from the Board of Trade, who examined the structure in March 1867. The rest of the bridge as far as the marshes at Morfa Mawddach comprises 113 wooden spans which are a clear favourite with local fishermen, whose rods jut out from the railings at irregular intervals. It is then just half a mile alongside BR's Cambrian Coast line to Morfa Mawddach station, where the Cambrian Railways' branch to Dolgellau – and the modern railway walk – begin.

Surveying the spartan facilities at Morfa Mawddach, it is hard to imagine

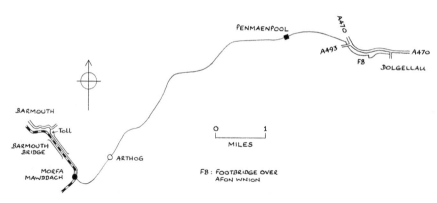

The Mawddach Estuary

that this was once a major triangular junction bordered by double track on all three sides. There were five platforms in total: two each for the Cambrian Coast and Ruabon lines, plus a bay platform which also faced Ruabon. The Cambrian Railways considered the junction important enough to be equipped with a refreshment room, but this has long gone; all that remains now are some public toilets and a small car park behind the single platform, and one suspects that these are more for the benefit of trail walkers than railway passengers.

The railway walk strikes off in a north-easterly direction, passing a small track at GR 630139 which I took to be the course of one of Solomon Andrews' Tramways. These tramways were built in the 1860s to transport materials needed for the construction of Barmouth Bridge; they ran from Tyddyn Sieffre Granite Quarry, across what is now the A493 (GR 630135), continuing past the east end of Barmouth Junction station to a reverse spur, where they ran back along the water's edge to reach the south end of the bridge. (A sketch map is provided in *Railways of the Wnion Valley and Mawddach Estuary*; see Bibliography.) The trail then continues along a shallow embankment for a mile before reaching the site of Arthog station at GR 641148.

Arthog was a late addition to the branch and was opened by the Cambrian Railways on 28 March 1870. Its facilities were somewhat basic, comprising a timber platform and single-storey building, whose only non-flammable portion was the corrugated iron roof. A long row of fire buckets on a railing outside reminded the staff of its vulnerability. The station also possessed a siding which, during the 1950s, became home to one of BR's popular camping coaches. Little remains of all this today, although the keen observer will find a series of concrete foundations set in the ground on the east side of the trackbed. These contain a number of old rails cut off at ground level, which once supported the station platform.

A modern view from the site of Arthog station, where stationmaster W.T. Edwards saved his life during a flood by clinging to a ground frame lever. The empty trackbed to Dolgellau can be seen disappearing into the distance

John Gibberd

Arthog station is followed by a long metal bridge which takes the line over a tributary of the Mawddach, after which it runs along a heavily engineered bank built up on the south side of the estuary. There are superb mountain views on all sides and, for once, no vegetation to obstruct them. The long bridge at GR 653161 is unusual as it retains a complete set of metal telegraph poles. Garth Sidings were situated hereabouts, although I could find no obvious trace of them; they were installed to serve a narrow gauge tramway that ran from nearby Tyn-y-Coed Quarry. Another sizeable bridge, of three-span metal girder construction, is reached at GR 671176 and, three quarters of a mile later, the line turns inland through an avenue of trees. This brings the walker to the site of Penmaenpool station (GR 694184).

Penmaenpool station is a very interesting location for the railway walker. Surviving features include the stationmaster's house, the signal protecting the nearby level-crossing, the station nameboard and the signal-box, now used by the RSPB as a visitor and information centre. The presence of the

Penmaenpool signal-box has found a new lease of life as an RSPB visitor and information centre. It was restored during the winter of 1992–3 when the RSPB discovered that it was a prototype built for the Great Exhibition of 1851. With its large observation windows, once used by railwaymen to keep a watchful eye on passing trains, it now makes an excellent, weatherproof refuge from which to view the local wildlife.

Author

RSPB here is hardly surprising, for the estuary supports a wide variety of bird life including buzzards, herons, ringed plovers, curlews and oystercatchers. The observation window of the signal-box is an excellent vantage point from which to study the wildlife, and, of course, it is fully insulated from the vicissitudes of the weather outside. According to one of the RSPB volunteers, the box was the prototype of a style used extensively throughout the GWR and was developed for the Great Exhibition of 1851; its pedigree had only just been discovered, and it was this that prompted its wholesale restoration during the winter of 1992–3.

Apart from the railway remains, the other obvious feature at Penmaenpool is the trestle toll bridge which carries a minor road over the river to Borthwnog. This was opened in 1879 to replace an earlier ferry and was later acquired by the Cambrian Railways. It is the lowest road crossing of the Afon Mawddach and was no doubt encouraged by the existence of gold mines on the north side of the river; these have now all closed but there was something of a gold rush here between 1902 and 1904, at which time the local mines employed over 500 men. The road on to the bridge bumped over the railway via a level-crossing, immediately east of which stood the two timber platforms of Penmaenpool station, together with a small goods yard and loading dock. Most of this has disappeared without trace, buried beneath a modern car

Old picture, new frame. An original station sign, mounted on a new board, still oversees comings and goings at Pemmaenpool thirty years after the last train departed

Author

park, but the foundations of the Up platform could be seen a few years ago half buried in mud at the water's edge.

Beyond Penmaenpool, the trail continues east through an avenue of trees before reaching a bridge over a marsh at GR 705186; there is a sluice on the north side of this, which presumably acts as a barrier against rising salt water. Another large bridge, festooned with notices from the local angling club, follows at GR 713183. By this time, the railway has left the valley of the Afon Mawddach for that of the Afon Wnion which it followed for 7 miles to Drws-y-Nant, just short of the summit between Dolgellau and Bala. Soon, however, the trail reaches the A493, for road improvements have obliterated the trackbed all the way through Dolgellau and a diversion is necessary to avoid a busy section of dual carriageway. Cross the road bearing slightly to the right and climb over a stile which gives access to a path along the north bank of the Afon Wnion. Follow this as far as GR 722179, where an attractive footbridge carries the path to the opposite bank. Once over the bridge, turn left and continue straight ahead to the main car park in Dolgellau, which is situated at the north end of Bridge Street (GR 728179). Throughout this section – an agreeable riverside walk – the old railway is never more than a few hundred yards away to the north, but most walkers will be pleased to be some distance from the traffic which now roars along it.

Dolgellau is a picturesque market town characterized by narrow streets and granite buildings; to reach it, turn right on leaving Bridge Street Car Park. If you want to see the remains of Dolgellau station, turn left instead and proceed across the bridge (Bont Fawr) to a T junction. Turn left here into Barmouth Road and proceed as far as the Police Station on your right, after which the old station yard will be found on your left (GR 725181). The site is now used by Dolgellau Farmers: the weighbridge and weighbridge office survive, together with the base of one of the signal-boxes – not much to show for the extensive facilities that once stood here.

Further Explorations

There are no other official railway walks close at hand, although much of the trackbed to Bala remains intact together with no less than ten river bridges. Farmers have taken over a few sections as farm tracks but, generally, the only users are the local sheep. At Bala, a heavily engineered line to Trawsfynydd and Blaenau Ffestiniog struck off to the north: much of this remains intact, especially around Cwm Prysor where the engineering and scenery are breathtaking. There have been calls for this to be converted into an official trail, but so far they have all fallen on deaf ears. Only at Morfa Mawddach does a real opportunity arise, for here one could spend a morning or afternoon exploring the remains of Solomon Andrews' Tramways, much of which appears to have been incorporated in the local network of minor roads and footpaths.

Perhaps the paucity of railway walks is not surprising when one considers just how many local railways are still operating. Narrow gauge lines are well represented here: the Bala Lake, Corris, Fairbourne and Talyllyn railways are all within easy reach, and just south of the Corris Railway on the A478, the Centre for Alternative Technology is worth a look. On the face of it, this doesn't have a great deal to do with railway walks, although it does include a water-powered funicular railway. It also includes working demonstrations of many alternative technologies, which should interest readers of this book given that disused railways offer a valuable opportunity to create a transport network which is not based on the ever-increasing use of fossil fuels.

Transport and Facilities

Maps: Ordnance Survey: Landranger Series Sheet 124

Buses: Crosville Wales, Park Avenue,
             Aberystwyth, Dyfed, SY23 1PG
             Telephone: Aberystwyth (0970) 617951

             Gwynedd County Council, Planning Department,
             County Offices, Caernarfon, Gwynedd, LL55 1SH
             Telephone: Caernarfon (0286) 679378

Trains: British Rail Telephone Enquiry Bureau
             Telephone: Shrewsbury (0743) 364041

It doesn't really matter where you start this walk, as both ends are well served by public transport. At the western end, Barmouth and Morfa Mawddach have a slight advantage by virtue of their stations on BR's scenic Cambrian Coast line, but Dolgellau also has good bus services westwards along both sides of the Mawddach Estuary. The service to Barmouth is best with a bus roughly every hour until about 8.00 p.m. (route 37), but there are also about six buses a day to Morfa Mawddach, Fairbourne and beyond (route 28). The winter services are slightly reduced and Sunday buses throughout the year are virtually non-existent, but a few Dolgellau–Barmouth journeys may be operated on Sundays during the school summer holidays. The advice offered in the previous chapter still holds good: if you are thinking of using these services, get a copy of the free county-wide timetable from Gwynedd County Council.

The pub situation is pretty good too, with a wide choice of hostelries in both Barmouth and Dolgellau. Collectively, they offer a decent range of beers from Birmingham and the north-west, including Ansells, Burtonwood and Robinsons. Mention must also be made of the seventeenth-century George Hotel at Penmaenpool, which is admirably convenient being on the trail itself. When I visited, the lower bar (facing the river) served a first-class pint of Marston's Pedigree and a wonderful selection of buffet-style salads (you buy a savoury and then serve yourself). This is just the sort of place to make you think the best of railway rambling, especially after travelling both ways along the trackbed as I had done. Every railway walk should have one.

4
THE ELAN VALLEY

Elan Valley Visitor Centre to Craig Goch Reservoir

Introduction

One of the delights of exploring disused railways in Wales is the variety of different types of line that one encounters. Rural branches and the occasional secondary main line are predictable stuff, but plateways, tramways and narrow gauge lines are out of the ordinary. This chapter goes one step further by offering walkers the opportunity to explore a nineteenth-century contractor's railway.

The scenery through which it passes in the remote Elan Valley is some of the finest in mid Wales, and it is hardly surprising that the area forms part of the Cambrian Mountains Environmentally Sensitive Area. However, no such designation existed when the engineers of Birmingham Corporation designed and built the massive dams which now give the valley its aquatic nature. There were protests against their construction, of course, not least at the loss of two large houses which had literary connections with the poet Shelley, but many locals felt that the development of reservoirs here was inevitable sooner or later. It must also be admitted that the corporation graced the valley with some very fine civil engineering, whose style is known as 'Birmingham Baroque' to this day. A visit will quickly reveal why the dams and reservoirs, as well the mountain scenery, have become an attraction in their own right.

History

The Elan Valley Railway was constructed to help build the chain of reservoirs which now supply Birmingham and the surrounding area with its daily water requirements. In the late nineteenth century, Birmingham was expanding at a tremendous rate and its demand for water doubled from 8.3 million gallons per day in 1876 to 16.5 million gallons in 1891. However, the local wells and springs could supply a maximum of only 18 million gallons per day, so the city was very close to the limit. Proposals to solve this problem by creating a series of reservoirs in the Elan Valley had been examined in 1871, although they were not progressed at this time; but by 1891, the situation had become urgent and this forced decisive action. (Interestingly, one of the factors which accelerated the Birmingham scheme was the realization that, if the city fathers did not act quickly, some other large city such as London might secure the same area for water storage instead.)

As a result, James Mansergh was appointed consultant engineer and asked to survey and report on the area concerned. His report was presented to the City of Birmingham Water Committee on 8 January 1891, officially approved in October and then used as the basis of the city's Water Bill, which received the Royal Assent on 27 June 1892. The resultant Act authorized the purchase of 71 square miles of 'gathering grounds' in the Elan and Claerwen Valleys; the construction of no less than six reservoirs; the establishment of a model village for the navvies; the construction of a 73 mile aqueduct to a new reservoir at Frankley, near King's Norton; and the construction of all the railways necessary for building and maintaining the dams.

The water committee moved fast. By the end of July 1893, all the land required for the railway had been purchased and Henry Lovatt of Wolverhampton was awarded the contract for constructing the permanent way – an inappropriate name in this case, as some of the lines were moved on an almost weekly basis! Lovatt had worked on many contracts of a similar size for companies such as the Great Northern, Midland, Great Western and Great Eastern railways, and his financial propriety was well known locally. Lovatt signed the contract on 29 September 1893 and, within two months, had staged a trial run by a locomotive over the first mile of track from the junction with the Cambrian Railways' Mid-Wales line to Aberceithon. This was the start of No. 1 Railway, which by spring 1894 had advanced as far as the site of Caban Coch Dam. In early July, Major Yorke, the Railway Inspector from the Board of Trade, approved the junction with the Mid-Wales line and, on 10 July, the first visit by an official party from Birmingham took place. (After all, the ratepayers from that city were financing the whole enterprise!)

In due course, No. 1 Railway was extended to the site of Dolymynach Dam (which, interestingly, was never completed), while No. 2, 3 and 4 Railways were also laid. No. 2 Railway ran from Caban Coch to Carreg-ddu and was started in late 1893; No. 3 Railway ran from Carreg-ddu to

Pennygarreg Dam in full spate, viewed from the trackbed of No. 4 Railway. Note the architectural style of the tower, known affectionately as 'Birmingham baroque', which is typical of the engineering works throughout the Elan Valley. Would civil engineers build something as elegant for similar public works today?

Author

Holywell Town station once stood in a deep man-made hollow, but the site has now been regraded, presumably to prevent earth slippage. The passenger platform was situated on the left in front of the bridge, while the stonework visible through the arch is a retaining wall at the foot of the former goods yard

Author

Lôn Eifion is the name given to the cycle trail built on the former LNWR line from Caernarfon to Afon Wen. A series of 'North Wales Land Cruises' travelled this way between 1951 and 1961 – it is easy to see why these trains were so popular. Today only walkers and cyclists can enjoy these views

Author

Pennygarreg and was laid during 1895; while No. 4 Railway ran from Pennygarreg to Craig Goch and was laid during 1896. It is impossible to give any precise dates for these lines as, once the main work on the dams began, a lot of railway detail disappeared from the water committee's minutes. However, by July 1896, trains could travel all the way from Elan Valley Railway Junction to the site of Craig Goch Dam.

At the height of the construction work, there were about 33 miles of track in the valley covering some 9 miles of route. Railways went everywhere: some of the dams, such as Caban Coch, even had temporary lines built near the top of the sloping dam wall, supported on an elaborate system of timber cantilevers. The Cambrian Railways did rather nicely out of the enterprise as well, for the quantity of inward freight was prodigious, particularly cement from the Medway area of Kent. For example, in the period up to January 1896, the Cambrian delivered 3,082 loaded wagons to the specially constructed interchange sidings at Neuadd. In order to handle this traffic, Birmingham Corporation acquired eight new saddle tanks from Manning Wardle and the Hunslet Engine Co., both of Leeds. It also purchased several hundred new and second-hand freight vehicles, as well as building many side-tip wagons on site in its workshops at Caban Coch. Finally, it also had a fleet of at least seventeen passenger coaches which were used to convey the navvies to the various construction sites, and their children to the local school.

With the exception of Lovatt's men, all of the navvies on this huge site were direct employees of Birmingham Corporation, a policy decided upon at the outset in order to avoid the 'scamping' that was epidemic with subcontractors – not to mention the frequent claims from their employers for 'extras' which had been overlooked in the original contract. By the standards of the time, the facilities provided for these men and their families were first class, a tribute to the social awareness of important Birmingham politicians such as Joseph Chamberlain. At a time when it was commonplace for single navvies to have to sleep twelve to a crowded dormitory, even the most lowly employee here was provided with his own cubicle. By 1898, the population of the model village had risen to 1,500, which made it larger than even neighbouring Rhayader. Its facilities were impressive: it included two hospitals, a chapel, police station, canteen, bath house, free library, Co-op stores and public hall. By 1896, a village fire brigade had been established and electricity had been installed in all the main buildings and streets; this was an early example of hydro-electric power, which remains in use to this day. By 1909, the original wooden buildings had been rebuilt permanently in stone.

As for the railway, its fate was inextricably linked with the continuation of construction work on the dams. Most of this had been completed by 1906, when the corporation sold its fleet of locomotives to Thomas W. Ward Ltd

Despite being nothing more than a contractor's line, the Elan Valley Railway was built to last. This bridge on the east side of Garreg-ddu Reservoir crosses a small stream which has dried up during the summer. The timber span is a recent addition by Welsh Water, but the masonry originates from the constrction of No. 3 Railway in 1895

John Gibberd

of Sheffield. The Cambrian Railways then operated the line for the rest of its life, although the traffic had dwindled to a monthly train to Caban Coch beyond which all the rails were lifted. The complex junction with the Cambrian's mid Wales line was simplified in 1908 to a siding controlled by a ground frame.

In 1916, the Cambrian carried out a survey of the branch and found that the line was 'out of repair'. It asked Birmingham Corporation to consider renewing it but, after due deliberation, the corporation decided to lift the track and realize its scrap value instead. On 14 October 1916, the Cambrian was informed that the line was being cut back to Neuadd Sidings and that all future rail deliveries were to be taken there for onward shipment by road. The traffic was now minimal and comprised only chalk for the filter beds at Elan Village plus a small amount of coal; the combined weight came to about 55 tons per month. On 15 January 1917, the Cambrian tested a six coupled goods engine as far as Neuadd, but the traffic was now in terminal decline: only six journeys were made that year, the last one running on 14 May 1917. Most corporation traffic was now going by road and this pattern was continued in the 1950s when it built the massive Claerwen Dam three miles west of Dolymynach. No definite date can be found for the line's final closure.

To finish on a bright note, mention should be made of the royal visit by King Edward VII and Queen Alexandra on 21 July 1904, when the reservoirs were officially opened. Due to the tight curves on the Elan Valley Railway, the royal visitors (and all others for that matter) had to change trains at Rhayader, exchanging the comfort of modern bogie stock for a ride in an antiquated four-wheeler. At least the king and queen had a roof over their heads – most of the crowds had to travel in the corporation's open wagons, which had boards nailed across them to provide rudimentary seats. As befitted the occasion, the visitors were all turned out in their best clothing, and one can imagine their reaction when the train plunged into the dank single bore of Rhayader Tunnel. It was fortunate that the engines had spark arresters fitted!

The royal party stopped for a buffet lunch in a series of specially erected marquees by the filter beds in Elan Village before travelling on to Craig Goch Dam at the northern end of the line. There, the king and queen walked across the dam to inspect the work and enjoy the fine view to the south before returning to their train, which conveyed them back to Rhayader for a 3.15 p.m. departure to London. Along the way, the railway was lined by members of the Shropshire Light Infantry who presented arms as the king passed.

The Line Today

Although the Elan Valley Railway closed in 1917, its works were not subject to the usual depradations that befall abandoned railways. Birmingham Corporation and its successors continued to own the land over which the line ran, and the only intrusion it suffered was invasion by the occasional stray sheep. (Local sheep farming, incidentally, started in earnest over 800 years ago when the Elan Valley was given to the Cistercian monks of Strata Florida Abbey, who developed wool production into an international business.)

The four main lines were designed to end up about 13 ft above the final water line and, as a result, much of the network is still extant today. This includes a number of well-built masonry bridges, which until the late 1980s still possessed their original – if somewhat rotten – spans. Here and there, the sites of various turnouts, passing loops and sidings can also be seen.

Nowadays, the area is administered by Welsh Water which, with financial support from the Countryside Council for Wales, has developed the old line into a proper trail complete with waymarking, interpretive panels and an informative leaflet. It has also carried out a number of improvements, the most obvious being to replace the rotten spans on the bridges and install a number of picnic tables around Carreg-ddu.

The Walk (5½ Miles)

The walk starts on the north side of the Elan Valley Visitor Centre, which is situated at GR 928647; a convenient car park will be found nearby. In the mid 1890s, this area was a mass of railway sidings, with a timber trestle bridge at the west end spanning the River Elan and carrying No. 1 Railway up the Claerwen Valley to the construction site for Dolymynach Dam. All this is rather difficult to imagine now as one gazes around at one's fellow visitors, most of whom will have arrived by car.

The 'main' line ran above and behind the visitor centre on the south side of the minor road to Pont ar Elan (GR 903716). It can be reached via a zigzag path which starts behind the centre and climbs steeply uphill, reaching the trackbed of No. 2 Railway close to the point where a reverse spur led off to the filter bed construction site. For the walker, the worst exertions are now over and the trail can be followed easily all the way to Craig Goch Dam (GR 894687).

While the railway trackbed retains a number of interesting features, the most imposing sights are of the dams themselves. The first of these is Caban Coch, which is reached at GR 924645. This was not in spate when I visited and the large protruding stones on the front face of the dam were clearly visible; these are provided to break up the water as it falls and reduce the impact on the valley floor. Just to the east of the dam are two attractive turbine houses, connected by a triple-arched stone bridge. These provide electricity at 525 volts for use in the filter beds and at 220 volts for use in the village and nearby waterworks installations. This is a very early hydro-electric installation, for these turbine houses were lighting the village streets as long ago as 1896.

The line continues south-west alongside Caban Coch Reservoir, turning sharply north as it rounds Coed y Foel. This 1,400 ft mountain is penetrated by a 1½ mile tunnel which carries water from the Foel Tower (of which more later) to the filter beds in Elan village. As one rounds the corner, an attractive bridge comes into view which carries a minor road into the Claerwen Valley. However, looks here are deceptive; the bridge actually

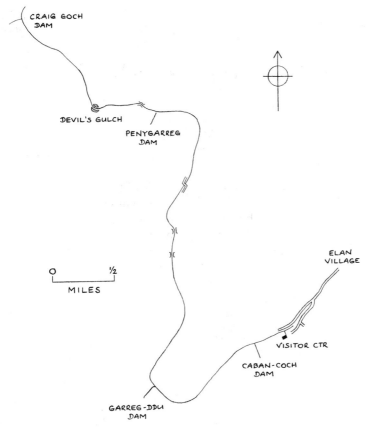

CRAIG GOCH
DAM

DEVIL'S GULCH

PENYGARREG
DAM

ELAN
VILLAGE

0   ½

MILES

VISITOR CTR

CABAN-COCH
DAM

GARREG-DDU
DAM

The Elan Valley

sits astride the submerged Garreg-ddu Dam, which was constructed to
maintain the level of water at the point where it is drawn off at the start of its
73 mile journey to Birmingham. The draw-off lies immediately beneath the
Foel Tower (GR 911641), which is actually a valve house capable of
drawing water from different depths of the reservoir. The valves here are
worked by hydraulic pressure at 700 lb to the square inch, which is
generated in the turbine houses at Caban Coch.

A brief detour across the bridge leads to Nantgwyllt Baptist church, built
to replace an earlier chapel used by the local farming community and now
buried beneath 90 ft of water. Despite the fact that the new church is barely
a century old, there have been serious problems with its maintenance: it is
not supplied with electricity, which does not reach this far up the valley, and
damp has affected the timber and internal decorations. Despite recent
renovation work, the foundations still need to be dried out, and the small

This is No. 4 Railway north of Devil's Gulch on the final approach to Craig Goch Dam. The empty trackbed looks as if it wouldn't take much to put the railway back

John Gibberd

congregation is trying to raise the many thousands of pounds needed for this. A small display of photographs at the end of the nave, showing the area before, during and after construction of the dams, is of historical interest.

Back on the trackbed, the line passes through a corridor of double railings by the Foel Tower, after which the now vanished Garreg-ddu Junction offered a choice of routes. No. 2 Railway originally forked left here and descended to the valley floor, while No. 3 Railway forked right and continued on to the base of Pennygarreg Dam, 2½ miles further north. This is the route that we must take today. However, before moving on, it is worth emphasizing just how many railways there once were in this vicinity. The valley floor was littered with sidings and reverse spurs that led south to a stone-breaking plant and sand crusher near Nantgwyllt Baptist church, while even the bridge across the reservoir once carried rails rather than tarmac.

No. 3 Railway heads off north along the east bank of Garreg-ddu Reservoir and soon parts company with the road to Pont ar Elan, which has accompanied the main line all the way from the filter beds in Elan Village.

This is a scenic section of the route, and Welsh Water has provided a number of picnic tables for those who wish to stop and admire the view. Two bridges with original stone abutments survive at GR 914657 and 914660, the latter being a particularly fine example of the contractor's work. Looking at the quality of the masonry, one would scarcely believe that this was part of a temporary railway. Until the late 1980s, these bridges also retained their original spans, but seventy years of non-maintenance had made them hazardous to cross; thankfully, the water company has now replaced them.

At GR 916665, the line crosses the road to Pont ar Elan at what looks suspiciously like a former level crossing. Do not be deceived; this is the site of Dolfaenog Junction, and it looks like a level crossing only because the trackbed of No. 3 Railway has been tarmacked over. Here the modern walker is confronted by a three-way choice: ignore the track on the right (this is a cul-de-sac anyway) and follow the path in the centre which leads off through a stand of fir trees. This is the start of No. 4 Railway, while the road on the left has been constructed on the empty bed of No. 3 Railway, which here began its descent to the construction site at the base of Pennygarreg Dam.

The old railway is now a bridleway and the gradient over the next mile is very pronounced. At GR 912675, the line passes within a few yards of the north end of Pennygarreg Dam, which offers some tremendous views when in spate. It then continues along the edge of Pennygarreg Reservoir, travelling first west and then north. At GR 910676, Nant Hesgog is crossed by a substantial bridge built with blue engineering bricks (wide enough for double track although this was never laid) before reaching the main feat of the line at GR 904676. This is Devil's Gulch, a nickname given by the navvies to a huge outcrop of rock through which, with picks and shovels, they carved a narrow passageway for the railway to travel. The result today is a dramatic man-made gorge with a towering rock wall on the north-east side. The line then continues north for another mile to Craig Goch Dam, where King Edward VII officially opened the Elan Valley Reservoirs on 21 July 1904. A branch to the base of the dam leaves the main line at GR 898684, passing through what is now a large picnic area.

At Craig Goch Dam, an open area on the left of the trail (GR 895687) marks the point where the king alighted from the royal train all those years ago. The memorial of his visit lies some miles to the south above the entrance door to the Foel Tower, although a public convenience has been added nearby for the benefit of lesser mortals. The top of the dam is crossed by a road, which offers magnificent views to the south. The railway continued for a few hundred yards in a north-easterly direction, but a modern bridleway follows a similar course and it is difficult to distinguish one from the other. I walked half a mile up to Rhiw Caws (GR 902690) and

Devil's Gulch is the main engineering feature on the Elan Valley Railway, and its excavation – entirely by pick and shovel – delayed the opening of No. 4 Railway by some three months. The tightness of the curve which necessitated check rails is still evident in this modern photograph

John Gibberd

then stopped to savour the view across Craig Goch Reservoir. What greeted me was a scene as tranquil and remote as one could hope to find anywhere in these crowded islands: no cars, no houses, no people, no sheep – only the empty slopes of green mountain tops stretching away as far as the eye could see.

Further Explorations

The most obvious other route to explore in this area is the course of No. 1 Railway, which ran from Tunnel Junction on the Cambrian's mid Wales line to Elan Village and Dolymynach Dam. Unfortunately, the trackbed from Rhayader to Elan Village is in private ownership, but a short length of the Dolymynach section can be walked between Caban Coch Dam and Nant y Gro (GR 925644 to 922635). This is not particularly easy, though, for the trackbed is rather rocky – do take care. I tried to tackle the line from the Dolymynach end, but though I had a great time rooting around in the undergrowth and found all sorts of intriguing industrial remnants, I would not wish to commit myself to a positive identification in print! It is possible that much of this line now lies beneath the waters of Caban Coch Reservoir, in which case one could only expect to identify it during a period of drought.

Other explorations in this area require a fair amount of travelling, a consequence of Powys County Council's apparent lack of interest in old railways. One interesting route lies over the border in Dyfed, near the little village of Pontrhydfendigaid. This was once the nearest settlement of any size to Strata Florida station on the extraordinary Manchester & Milford Railway. And this railway was extraordinary too; its ambitions were clearly laid out in its title, despite the engineering difficulties inherent in so vast a scheme, and the fact that it managed to raise only a fraction of its authorized capital. This is not the place to elaborate on the history of this fascinating if somewhat madcap scheme, but suffice it to say that the M&M built a line from Pencader to Strata Florida, where escalating problems forced it to turn left and head for Aberystwyth. (The resultant kink in the railway map of Wales remained a memorial to the M&M's failed ambitions for almost a century.) Fortunately, 2 miles of this historic route are now part of Cors Caron National Nature Reserve and can be walked officially: the trail begins from a car park near Maesllyn Farm on the B4343, 2 miles north of Tregaron, and continues to the observation tower in the middle of Cors Caron at GR 704647.

Transport history of a different kind beckons to the north-east of Rhayader at Newtown, for this is the southern terminus of the 35 mile

Montgomery Canal which starts at Frankton on the famous Llangollen Canal. The Montgomery is not currently navigable throughout, although the cut remains intact as far as the outskirts of Newtown, and the Montgomery Waterway Restoration Trust – actively supported by British Waterways – intends to reopen the entire line in due course. In 1987, British Waterways obtained an Act of Parliament authorizing the reopening and, the following year, a House of Commons Select Committee recommended that the route should be restored. A surprising amount of work has already been completed but, until the canal is fully operational again, the towpath offers a most acceptable way of exploring the attractive border country on foot.

Transport and Facilities

Maps: Ordnance Survey: Landranger Series Sheet 147
         Ordnance Survey: Pathfinder Series Sheet 969 (recommended)

Buses: Cross Gates Coaches Ltd
         Cross Gates, Llandrindod Wells, Powys, LD1 6RE
         Telephone: Penybont (0597) 851226 or 851207

         Postbus Passenger Service
         Either:
         Post Office, Llandrindod Wells, Powys
         Telephone: Llandrindod Wells (0597) 824114
         Or:
         Royal Mail Postbus Development Team, Burlington House,
         Burlington Street, Chesterfield, Derbyshire, S40 1RX
         Telephone: Chesterfield (0246) 556728

         Roy Brown's Coaches
         15 High Street, Builth Wells, Powys
         Telephone: Builth Wells (0982) 552597

         Powys County Council, Highways & Transportation,
         County Hall, Llandrindod Wells, Powys, LD1 5LG
         Telephone: Llandrindod Wells (0597) 826643

Trains: British Rail Telephone Enquiry Bureaux
         Telephone: Shrewsbury (0743) 364041
             or: Swansea (0792) 467777

Public transport in this area is quite thinly spread: you can get just about anywhere you want, but you do have to travel at the operator's times. The nearest railhead is Llandrindod Wells on BR's scenic mid Wales line from Llanelli to Shrewsbury, which enjoys a modest service of four trains per day in each direction. Buses from Llandrindod to Rhayader and the Elan Valley are provided by the three operators listed above.

Cross Gates Coaches provides a Mondays to Fridays service from Rhayader to Llandrindod for the benefit of county and district council office staff, which runs east in the mornings and west in the evenings. This is supplemented by extra journeys on Wednesdays, Fridays and Saturdays, with one of the Wednesday buses running through to Elan Village. Roy Brown also provides a single return journey from Rhayader to Llandrindod and Hereford on Mondays, Wednesdays, Fridays and Saturdays. This leaves Llandrindod Wells for Rhayader between 6.30 and 7.00 p.m. (depending on the day) and is useable by people arriving on the afternoon train – the two hour wait is a bit much, but at least there's no chance of missing the bus! Finally, on Mondays to Fridays the postbus makes two journeys from Llandrindod to Rhayader, one of which is extended to Elan Village. This last service runs to Craig Goch and Pont ar Elan on request. Needless to say, anyone thinking of using these services should check the details beforehand with the operator or the public transport staff at County Hall.

In so remote an area as this, one might have thought that pubs would be hard to come by, but this is not the case. Two hostelries are conveniently close to the walk, namely the Elan Valley Hotel in Elan Village (GR 938658) and the Flickering Lamp near Pennygarreg Dam (GR 915672). During the summer, a small car park about 100 yd below the Flickering Lamp also plays host to an ice cream van, which sells teas and coffees as well as the usual frozen confections. In nearby Rhayader, the situation is even better, for this small town has a number of good pubs offering a range of beers far wider than found in many places four or five times its size. The ancient Cornhill Inn in West Street is a particular favourite.

5
THE DYFED COAST

Johnston to Neyland and the Saundersfoot Railway

Introduction

In this chapter, we again have something rather different – the tail end of a main line from Paddington, built to convey passengers to the Irish steam packets, and a network of industrial lines around Saundersfoot, built to serve collieries in the former Daucleddau coalfield. Both lie within 10 miles of each other on the south coast of Dyfed, much of which now lies within the Pembrokeshire Coast National Park.

Both walks lie south of the A40 in an area known locally as 'Little England'. The countryside certainly has an English look about it, reminiscent of parts of the West Country or Shropshire, and many of the towns and villages have names which do not over-strain one's powers of pronunciation. The area's chief splendour is its coastal scenery, which can be enjoyed from the somewhat strenuous Pembrokeshire Coast Path. Many attempting this walk must be grateful for the level section between Saundersfoot Harbour and Wiseman's Bridge, but I expect that few realize as they climb above the cliffs once more that they have just been railway rambling . . .

History

A. Johnston to Neyland

The casual walker strolling down the empty trackbed of the railway from Johnston to Neyland might be forgiven for thinking that it was just another rural branch line, but for fifty years it was the western terminus of the South Wales Railway and, as such, received regular through trains from Paddington.

The SWR was authorized by an Act dated 4 August 1845 to build a line from near Gloucester to Fishguard, with a branch to Pembroke on the south side of Milford Haven. Anxious to tap the sea traffic with Ireland, the GWR was very supportive and in 1846 leased the company for a guaranteed 5 per cent dividend – provided it reached Fishguard. The SWR's main line opened from Chepstow to Swansea on 18 June 1850, with the Gloucester–Chepstow section following on 19 September 1851; the delay was caused by a difficult bridge over the River Wye at Chepstow. By this time, work west of Swansea had advanced to within 7 miles of Fishguard, but then the Irish economy collapsed in the wake of the 1851 famine. This meant that the SWR's partners in Ireland were unable to continue with developments on their side of the Irish Sea, and all work on the new line came to a complete stop leaving a tunnel and various bridges half built.

Unable to reach Fishguard, the management of the SWR cast about for an alternative harbour. The incomplete Fishguard line already extended from Swansea to a point west of Clarbeston Road, so the obvious solution was to turn south and develop a site on Milford Haven. The company's engineer, I.K. Brunel, might have been expected to head for Milford where extensive docks were being built by private enterprise, but in typically Brunelian fashion he chose Neyland instead, 4 miles east of Milford and across the water from Pembroke, whose branch the company had still not started to build. An Act dated 17 June 1852 authorized construction of a railway to Neyland and, towards this end, the company opened the Swansea–Carmarthen section of its main line on 11 October the same year. On 2 January 1854, trains began running from Carmarthen to Haverfordwest and, on 15 April 1856, they finally reached Neyland via a single broad gauge line. As a matter of interest, the original landing stage at Neyland was built on the pontoons used to construct Saltash Bridge, which carries the West of England main line from Devon into Cornwall; Brunel had these moved from the River Tamar to Milford Haven by sea.

These developments quickly established Neyland as the GWR's main port for Ireland, and some impressive rail services – including a through sleeper train from Paddington – duly followed. One odd feature of these early years was that, having selected Neyland as their port, the SWR and GWR were perversely reluctant to call it by its real name: it was initially named 'New Milford (Milford Haven)' before becoming plain 'New Milford'. Despite the anonymity created by the bogus name, Neyland enjoyed its pre-eminence for half a century, but on 30 August 1906, Fishguard Harbour finally opened with a new shipping service to Rosslare. The Fishguard–Rosslare crossing was 54 miles compared with the

Neyland–Waterford crossing of 98 miles, so it was fairly obvious what would happen. Neyland's trade quickly collapsed and, two years later, the Waterford sailings were also transferred to Fishguard, effectively finishing the town as a sea port, although at least the GWR then restored its rightful name.

Under normal circumstances, one might have expected the town and its railway to go into a steady decline, but Neyland survived remarkably well. It had a good freight traffic with outward fish and meat balancing inward coal, while its locomotive shed – which provided most of the motive power on both the Neyland and Fishguard branches – ensured that it was highly regarded by the GWR's timetabling staff. Perhaps this explains why it continued to enjoy a sleeper service to and from Paddington for over fifty years after it ceased to function as a passenger port! Given the small size of the town, an examination of old railway timetables is very instructive. In 1922, there were generally seven trains each way daily, with Paddington workings travelling either via Gloucester or the Severn Tunnel. Local trains ran to and from Bristol, Cardiff, Carmarthen, Clynderwen, Fishguard and Swansea. In 1953, the service was broadly similar although the daily sleeper service had been reduced to a single return working, out on Saturday and back on Sunday.

Unfortunately, the line then succumbed to the 1960s enthusiasm for road transport and, by the time Dr Beeching conducted his infamous review of British Railways, the Neyland line was a clear candidate for 'rationalization'. Goods facilities were withdrawn on 2 December 1963, with passenger closure following on 15 June 1964. Like so many other lines, it wasn't even allowed the dignity of a final summer season.

B. The Saundersfoot Railway

The Saundersfoot Railway & Harbour Company, to use its full title, operated a network of industrial lines around Saundersfoot with a unique gauge of 4 ft. (Although several sources record a slightly wider gauge, 4 ft was the official figure.) Until the company's appearance in 1829, the local coal industry had been relatively backward and complacent: most output was dispatched by sea, and ships were loaded either on the River Cleddau or from open beaches. As most of the mines were inland, this meant that considerable tonnages had to be moved by horse and cart, and local roads were badly damaged as a result. However, the start of anthracite mining in the Gwendraeth Valley east of Kidwelly created competition on an unprecedented scale, and it soon became clear that the local industry would have to improve or face the consequences. The two most obvious improvements were to provide a proper harbour and efficient transport facilities.

The Saundersfoot Railway and Harbour Company was proposed in 1828 with the twin aims of building a harbour at Saundersfoot and various

An historic view of The Strand, Saundersfoot, in its previous guise of Railway Street. The train is a miners' special *en route* to Stepaside hauled by the Saundersfoot Railway's 0–4–0 Manning Wardle locomotive. In a few yards, it will enter the first of three tunnels on what is now part of the Pembrokeshire Coast Path. These miners' expresses were discontinued after a coal strike in 1926

Lens of Sutton

connecting tramways to local collieries. It obtained its Act on 1 June 1829 and rapidly set about construction. Not surprisingly, the harbour opened first – in 1832 – after which the company turned its attention to railway building. Initially, the harbour was served only by a half mile branch from Coppet Hall, but by 1 March 1834, this had been extended to Wiseman's Bridge and the main line opened from the harbour to Thomas Chapel. The eastern section from Wiseman's Bridge to Lower Level Colliery at Kilgetty opened in February 1836 after a delay caused by storm damage.

The railway was single track throughout with a few passing loops, its principal engineering features being a 300 yd incline at Bonville's Court and no less than four tunnels. Three of these occurred on the coastal section between Saundersfoot and Wiseman's Bridge, while the fourth – and by far the longest – carried the main line under a hill near the appropriately named Hill hamlet. The track initially consisted of stone block sleepers bearing cast iron rails, but brittleness led to their partial replacement with wrought iron rails obtained from Bristol. The company's Act authorized locomotives provided they consumed their own smoke, an impossible condition which made the use of horses unavoidable. A further Act of 1842 granted powers for the conveyance of passengers, but these were never exercised except for the later 'Colliers' Expresses' which carried miners to and from work at the beginning and end of each day.

During the 1840s, many new pits were sunk locally and both railway and harbour reaped the benefits of increased trade. In 1846, the Pembrokeshire Coal and Iron Company was established, which three years later opened a new ironworks at Stepaside – the first serious attempt to improve the local iron industry. The ironworks, served by a branch from the existing line to Kilgetty, soon established a reputation for quality and became the most important terminal on that route. For a time, the works also built steam engines, one of which was installed in the winding house at the top of Bonville's Court Incline where it remained until 1930.

On 4 September 1866, the Pembroke & Tenby Railway opened its broad gauge line from Whitland to Tenby, establishing an exchange siding with the Saundersfoot Railway just south of its new Saundersfoot station (which, incidentally, was built over the southern end of Hill Tunnel). A physical link between the two systems was out of the question due to the different gauges, but this facility appears to have been used until 1893, when the P&TR (then worked by the Great Western) closed the exchange siding and opened a direct branch into Bonville's Court Colliery. This shrewd manoeuvre effectively cut out the middle man and diverted 50 per cent of the colliery's output straight on to GWR metals.

In many ways, the arrival of the P&TR marked the start of a downturn in the fortunes of the Saundersfoot Railway. It appears not to have suffered unduly from competition – apart from the Bonville's Court incident – but it could hardly prosper if its customers went out of business; yet this is precisely what happened. Kilgetty and Grove collieries closed in 1870 and 1873 respectively, and pig iron production stopped at Stepaside in 1874 following a strike. At about the same time, the line from Saundersfoot station to Thomas Chapel was abandoned, implying that traffic had also ceased from Broom and Thomas Chapel collieries. Despite these ominous signs, the company chose 1874 to relay its line from Saundersfoot Harbour to Stepaside with flat-bottomed rails spiked on to conventional transverse wooden sleepers. Powers were then obtained to run steam locomotives on this section, after which a Manning Wardle 0–4–0 saddle tank was acquired. This was housed in a wooden shed at Stepaside, where a stone maintenance building was also erected. The company was rewarded for these endeavours in 1877 when Stepaside Ironworks closed completely, unable to continue in the face of foreign competition.

Further colliery closures followed, with Moreton going in 1887 and Lower Level at Kilgetty in 1900. This left Bonville's Court as the only colliery of any significance in the whole Saundersfoot area. Fortunately, mechanical aids had been installed here at the end of the nineteenth century, and these led to large productivity increases: in 1925, for example, output from Bonville's Court represented 82 per cent of the total for the whole of Pembrokeshire.

By 1914, the casual observer might have thought that the Saundersfoot Railway was near the end, but the advent of World War I increased the nation's demand for coal and turned the company around. A new pit was sunk at Reynalton, and in 1915 a railway connection was provided by means of a 1½ mile extension from Thomas Chapel. New track was laid from the top of the incline to Reynalton using flat-bottomed rail and transverse wooden sleepers (thus reviving a section that had long been abandoned), and a new Kerr Stuart 0–4–0 saddle tank *Bull Dog* was purchased to handle the traffic. This was an odd looking locomotive to say the least, for its height was only 6 ft and even this left only 6 in clearance through Hill Tunnel. Due to the incline at Bonville's Court, the railway was operated in two distinct sections, with *Bull Dog* working traffic from Reynalton to the top of the incline, and the Manning Wardle locomotive working traffic in the harbour and along the coast to Wiseman's Bridge.

However, the revival was to prove no more than an Indian summer, for in 1921 Reynalton Colliery closed, largely as a result of serious labour problems. The line beyond the top of the incline was then abandoned, for all the collieries along its route had ceased to provide any traffic. *Bull Dog* was transferred to Bonville's Court Colliery, but even this had only another nine years to run, closing in 1930. By April that year, all sources of traffic along the line had closed and the Saundersfoot Railway was moribund.

Amazingly, a revival came a few years later following the reopening of several local collieries, brought about partly, it would seem, by French customers who had received anthracite from Saundersfoot. Broom Colliery (near Thomas Chapel) reopened in January 1933 and produced its first coal in 1934. The railway responded by reconditioning and repainting its two locomotives, and reopening the line from Saundersfoot Harbour to the colliery in early 1935. Kilgetty Colliery reopened in the same year, but the eastern branch was not revived until 1936 as repairs were necessary following rock falls and storms along the coastal section.

Output from the reopened collieries was impressive with Broom producing 30,000 tons per annum between 1935 and 1938, but the revival was short lived due to geological and possibly financial problems. Kilgetty Colliery closed in February 1939 and all other local collieries had suffered the same fate by August that year. With nothing left to carry, the Saundersfoot Railway now closed for good.

The Lines Today

After closure, the Johnston–Neyland line remained in BR ownership and was left to languish until 1982, when most of it was purchased by Preseli

Pembrokeshire District Council. The council's deal with BR included acquisition of Neyland station and Brunel Quay, both of which were subsequently redeveloped. The trackbed was acquired at the same time because local people had been using it as a footpath since closure and no other reasonable use could be envisaged. In 1991, the council made a concerted effort to tidy up the route and began by running a bulldozer along it to remedy twenty-eight years' growth of vegetation – a drastic but effective solution to an old problem! It then cut back the remaining vegetation and installed a series of access controls and stiles to prevent unauthorized use by motor cyclists and horse riders. (The latter restriction raises hackles locally but is necessary to prevent damage to the trail surface.) The only trouble spot was the last half mile at the Johnston end which BR retained, thereby preventing the establishment of a proper link to the village. However, the council purchased this section for £300 in November 1993 and intends to have a connection open for public use by the end of 1994.

Despite its earlier closure, the fate of the Saundersfoot Railway is broadly similar. The track was dismantled and sold for scrap shortly after the start of World War II, while the rolling stock (consisting entirely of coal drams) was broken up at Bonville's Court along with the Manning Wardle locomotive. Being relatively new, the Kerr Stuart engine *Bull Dog* was sold to Llanelly Steelworks where it lasted until 1951. The trackbed from Saundersfoot to Wiseman's Bridge was remade as a footpath, while other sections (notably Wiseman's Bridge to Stepaside, King's Moor to Thomas Chapel and Bonville's Court Incline) were absorbed into the local footpath network. I cannot find a date for this, but it is hardly a surprising fate given that pedestrians frequently used the railway as a footpath even when it was operating. The only sections to escape reuse were the Reynalton extension and a one mile length including Hill Tunnel. The tunnel is still there beneath the south end of Saundersfoot station, but the approach cuttings are very overgrown and the tunnel itself is very wet. Near the northern end, it includes another tunnel off to the west but I have no idea how this came to be there.

The Saundersfoot Railway & Harbour Company continued to exist by virtue of Saundersfoot Harbour, but it was superseded – if not wound up – in 1958 when the government of the day created a body of Harbour Commissioners. In recent years, the Saundersfoot Steam Railway has been established at Stepaside (now being revived as a heritage centre) and this plans to build a 15 in narrow gauge line from Stepaside to Wiseman's Bridge. The line will be only a mile long, but it necessitated a public inquiry organized by the Railway Inspectorate, followed by an Act of Parliament! One of the conditions imposed upon the company is that it rebuilds the rather boggy public footpath along this section.

Walk 1 – Johnston to Neyland (4½ miles)

Access to the northern end of this walk is currently difficult but this problem should be resolved by the end of 1994 (see above). Starting at Johnston railway station (a depressing and spartan place), proceed up the station approach road to the A4076 and there turn right. Continue towards the village church and turn left at GR 932104 into the lane to Rosemarket. Greenhall Park is the first turning off this lane on the right: follow it as far as a left-hand bend, continuing straight ahead on to a track that leads downhill towards the site of Milford Haven Branch Junction (GR 936102). Here access on to the old trackbed should be easy but, alas, it is not; two locked

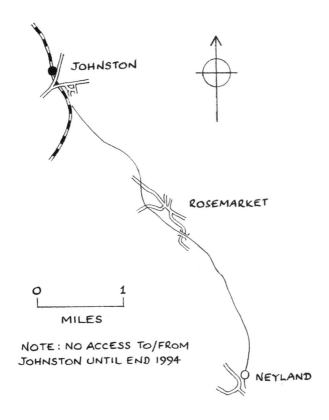

Johnston to Neyland

At the top of Bonville's Court Incline, Saundersfoot, the old winding house which hauled wagons between the company's two levels still survives. Until 1930, it accommodated a stationery engine built at Stepaside Ironworks

John Gibberd

gates either side of a privately-owned field bar the way and, even if you cross them, there is no simple way on to the Neyland branch beyond. Here lies the problem; in order to bypass the obstruction and reach the railway path, it is necessary to climb over the BR boundary fence on your right and walk alongside the operational Milford Haven line for a few yards. While this is easy and a route clearly used by locals, it involves trespassing on BR land and risking a fine of £200 – not a course of action to be recommended. Until the new link is in place, you are therefore advised to join the trail near Rosemarket (see below).

The north end of the branch is flanked by mature trees and bushes, which have the unfortunate effect of disguising an embankment with attractive views over a small valley to the left. Knowing that improvements are planned here, I will not describe my epic battle with nature but merely offer the hope that the council cuts some 'windows' in the vegetation so that walkers can enjoy the surrounding scenery. By the time the power lines at GR 945093 are passed, the shrubbery has begun to thin out and the walk is becoming more open. Looking down the broad sweep of the gentle curves that follow, one soon realizes that this was engineered as a main line rather than some rural outpost built on the cheap. What appears to be a crossing-keeper's cottage survives at GR 948086. This is followed by an attractive rock cutting, incised vertically into the hillside; the west wall of this supports a vigorous growth of blackberries, which were being harvested by several pickers as I passed.

The trail continues to skirt around Rosemarket, which never received a station despite its close proximity; perhaps the main line origins of the route blinded the railway authorities to its traffic potential. Another level crossing is passed at GR 949083, preceded by a large car park where one first encounters signs proclaiming this to be the 'Westfield Trail'. The path has now widened considerably and it appears that the formation was originally built for double track, although the 1952 Ordnance Survey map shows only a single line in place.

Though little remains of Neyland station, the finely proportioned stationmaster's house survives as a private residence. The modern satellite dish provides a stark reminder that much has changed since trains from Paddington arrived here to meet the Irish steam packets. (Please note that this is private property and not open to the public)

John Gibberd

The lane from Rosemarket to Neyland is crossed at GR 956077, a nasty spot for motorists who come face to face with a substantial railway bridge in the middle of a blind double bend. At GR 962073, the line passes Westfield Mill Crossing, from which the trail presumably takes its name. There is a long, modern-looking bungalow alongside the line here which may once have been a crossing-keeper's cottage. Certainly the lintel above the front door suggests this, and a GWR-style sign reading 'WESTFIELD MILL CROSSING' affixed to the nearby wall increases one's suspicions. The mill, presumably, was situated at the head of the nearby creek, but no trace of it is visible from the trackbed – if, indeed, it still survives.

The views begin to widen out as the line continues south along the western edge of the estuary, crossing a short causeway before passing under the towering A477 road bridge at GR 968060. Near this bridge, the estuary has been blocked by a weir which accounts for the high water level in the upper part of the creek, and signs indicate that the area is being managed by

The elaborate trackwork at Neyland is all that remains of the town's former station, yard and quay, but it is an unusual relic for all that. It was evidently cheaper to fill the rails with tarmac than remove them

John Gibberd

Dyfed Wildlife Trust as a nature reserve. By now, the view southwards is dominated by the masts of Neyland Marina, which has over 300 berths for yachts and cruisers. The Irish steam packets may have gone, but this lot should guarantee the town plenty of business! The trail finishes by the southern end of the marina, but the course of the railway can be traced as a new road which passes a row of modern executive houses.

In Neyland, the railway occupied a long, wide site alongside the estuary. This has been redeveloped as a small industrial estate with a predictable leaning towards marine activities. If at this point you find yourself following a new road on the right of the site, turn left and continue walking alongside the water. This will bring you on to Brunel Quay, where all the trackwork south of the station remains *in situ*, albeit now set in tarmac. There is some impressive pointwork here, including a pair of double slips. The railway ended by the site of Neyland Pier, which had just been demolished when I visited; its massive timbers, much corroded by salt water and marine plants, were piled up nearby in a large heap, and it looked as though the area was being redeveloped as a small waterside park.

To reach Neyland town centre, turn right and follow the old pier access road as far as the B4325 opposite Station House (GR 966049). Turn right again for the town centre, which has all the usual facilities plus buses to Rosemarket. Station House was formerly the stationmaster's residence; it is built on the site of a row of cottages which were demolished to make way for it. Unfortunately, little else remains to indicate that a large railway community used to exist here. In the words of James Page, 'This once proud and busy terminus has been laid flat, and the whistle shrieks that heralded the departure of the 1 p.m. to London, the 9.00 a.m. railmotor to Clarbeston Road, or a shunting movement in the sidings no longer startle the seagulls.'

Walk 2 – Stepaside to Saundersfoot and Ridgeway (3 miles)

This walk may be picked up at Stepaside Heritage Park (GR 138077). This is rather an awkward place to find as the narrow valley is fairly cluttered with lanes, but there are signs to the centre from the nearby A477, which passes within a quarter of a mile. Signs to the Saundersfoot Steam Railway are also a useful guide, as this is located on the same site.

The steam railway currently runs on an oval track which encircles vehicles left in the centre's car park. However, this is only a temporary arrangement, for the track will eventually be relaid along the course of the original

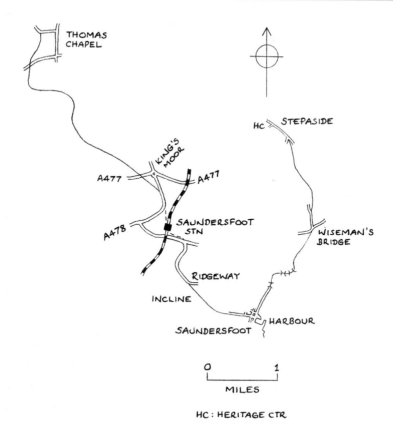

HC : HERITAGE CTR

The Saundersfoot Railway

Saundersfoot Railway from Stepaside to the coast at Wiseman's Bridge, a distance of just over a mile (see *The Lines Today*). This will make the accompanying footpath extremely obvious, but in the meantime, it is easily found. Imagine you are leaving the interpretive centre, turn left and proceed to the lane which runs alongside the site on its east side. Go out into the lane, turn right and proceed past the entrance to the car park. A few yards further on, again on the right-hand side, a waymarked path leads off through an avenue of trees (GR 142074). This is the course of the Saundersfoot Railway.

The path offers an attractive, silvan route to Wiseman's Bridge, and is extremely well used. It is accompanied for most of its distance by a small stream, which it crosses via a culvert at GR 143070. Half a mile later at GR 144063, the path emerges on to a narrow lane which then occupies the trackbed as far as the coast. Even this lane is of railway origin, for it was once the site of a passing loop; nearby Tramway Cottage confirms the connection.

On reaching the coastal road, walkers should cross over bearing right to pick up the Pembrokeshire Coast Path. This is a superbly constructed route, finished with a top dressing of rolled limestone dust. It is clearly well able to withstand the large number of walkers and bathers who use it, although possibly not the winter storms which are something of a problem here. The path now proceeds south, passing a man-made opening on the right (sealed off with a metal safety fence) before plunging into the first of three tunnels. This piece of engineering firmly dispels any doubts that the route was once the permanent way of a railway. The low height of this and other tunnels on the line is explained by the fact that the 'trains' originally consisted of coal drams pulled by horses; their small dimensions later dictated the size of the company's steam locomotives.

After emerging from the first tunnel, the longest on the line, the path quickly passes through the second, which is the shortest. It then skirts

This tunnel on the coastal section of the former Saundersfoot Railway between Wiseman's Bridge and Saundersfoot now forms part of the Pembrokeshire Coast Path. Even if one disregards the modern lining, its proportions were very small, necessitating the use of a diminutive locomotive without a cab

John Gibberd

around the right-hand side of a large car park before entering the third tunnel. If in doubt as to the correct route here, aim for the toilet block on the far side of the car park and the portal of the third tunnel will be seen to its left. This is clearly the most heavily used of all the tunnels, for it is equipped with street lighting. It emerges into The Strand, Saundersfoot, a name which rather disguises its history; in the nineteenth century it was called Railway Street. The line ran down the middle of the road to the harbour, where sidings fanned out on to both of the quays. While in the harbour area, it is worth noting the Raj Tandoori Restaurant/Barbecue Fish and Chip shop; this was formerly the harbour office.

The branch to Thomas Chapel started on the south quay and turned left into Milford Street. It then continued along Brooklands Place before reaching the foot of Bonville's Incline. This is now a public footpath which leads to a rather busy lane at Ridgeway (GR 127053). The incline had a gradient of 1 in 8 and rose about 100 ft in 300 yd; it is still quite a haul, even for an experienced and healthy walker. Although the track appeared to be double, the two lines actually shared a common middle rail. It was also 'self-

The modern Saundersfoot Steam Railway based at Stepaside is a somewhat different affair to its predecessor. It has a gauge of 15 in rather than 4 ft, and is in business to haul passengers rather than coal. When complete, it will run along the course of the earlier line between Stepaside and Wiseman's Bridge, giving visitors the chance to ride as well as walk part of this historic railway

Author

acting', which is to say that loaded wagons going down hauled up empties travelling the other way. There was, of necessity, a passing loop in the middle where the triple-railed section bowed outwards into a short length of conventional double track.

A great surprise lies at the top of Bonville's Incline, for the winding house still survives, although it has now been out of use for over fifty years. It must be admitted that it is not in good condition: it has lost its roof, and vandals have doubtless loosened and removed a number of stones from its walls. However, it is remarkable that it has survived at all in the face of such prolonged neglect.

Unfortunately, the top of the incline is where the walker must stop, for this is Ridgeway – our terminus – and it is not really practicable to go any further. In years gone by, the railway accompanied the road beyond as far as a T junction with the B4316 at GR 126058. This junction was the site of a level-crossing, where the railway turned west on its final approach to Hill Tunnel. On the map, it looks as though the road might be a quiet country lane, but it has a steady flow of traffic which can be rather hair-raising on the bends. If you must walk this section, please take extreme care. However, my advice would be to turn round and go back to Saundersfoot – there is no pleasure to be gained from near misses with speeding cars.

Further Explorations

The only other railway walk in this area is the continuation of the Saundersfoot Railway, which offers a further 2¼ miles of walking from a point on the A478 just south of King's Moor roundabout (GR 122067) to the little village of Thomas Chapel (GR 103089). All of this is a public footpath, but there is a gypsy camp *en route* at GR 118069 around which it might be judicious to make a diversion, while at least one person hangs washing across the line! This recalls the days when housewives performed the same trick across little-used colliery lines in the valleys, much to their cost if an unexpected train happened to come along. Further walking is available on the Pembrokeshire Coast Path, of course, but parts of this are no easy stroll.

The other attraction for those with an interest in transport and industrial archaeology is Stepaside Heritage Park. The buildings on this 15 acre site originate from Stepaside Ironworks and Grove Colliery, and include the course of a narrow gauge incline by which coal was lowered from the pithead down to a siding on the Saundersfoot Railway. The work here is being co-ordinated by the Stepaside Industrial Heritage Project, whose first task was to record the surviving buildings. In future, it may be able to restore some of them, including the ironworks cast-house, and the colliery engine-house and office.

Overall, Dyfed County Council has been indifferent about disused railways within its boundary, which is a great pity as an excellent opportunity presented itself in 1973 when British Rail closed the long-surviving freight line from Carmarthen to Newcastle Emlyn. This line may not be a railway walk but its spectacular scenery was not lost on steam preservationists, who have since opened two railways along its course. The first, the standard gauge Gwili Railway, has a Light Railway Order authorizing 8 miles of track between Bronwydd Arms (near Carmarthen) and Pencader, while the narrow gauge Teifi Valley Railway has purchased 9 miles of line between Pencader and Newcastle Emlyn. It is currently operating from Henllan, between the two.

Transport and Facilities

Maps: Ordnance Survey: Landranger Series Sheet 158

Buses: Silcox Motor Coach Company
           Waterloo Garage, Pembroke Dock, Dyfed
           Telephone: Pembroke (0646) 683143

           South Wales Transport, Withybush Road
           Industrial Estate, Haverfordwest, Dyfed
           Telephone: Haverfordwest (0437) 763284

           Dyfed County Council, Public Transport Section,
           Highways & Transportation, 8 Spilman Street,
           Carmarthen, Dyfed, SA31 1JY
           Telephone: Carmarthen (0267) 231817 (direct line)

Trains: British Rail Telephone Enquiry Bureau
           Telephone: Swansea (0792) 467777

The quickest and easiest way to find out about current bus services in Dyfed is to contact the county council's Public Transport Section (see above), which publishes a series of free route maps and timetables covering the whole of the county.

There is a two-hourly bus service from Neyland to Rosemarket, but no service at all between Neyland and Johnston; if you wish to make this journey, you must travel via Milford Haven using Silcox service 356 (approximately hourly until 5.30 p.m.) and SWT service 302 (at least hourly until 11.40 p.m.). There are no buses on any of these routes on Sundays. Until there is proper access to the trail at Johnston, I would suggest starting at Rosemarket: take a bus to Neyland, walk back to Rosemarket, then explore the northern section on an 'out and back' basis if you have time and the inclination. The car park at GR 949083 could serve as a convenient base.

The most useful services in the Saundersfoot area are the Silcox/SWT routes 350 and 351, which link Stepaside, Wiseman's Bridge, Kilgetty and Saundersfoot. There is generally at least one bus per hour until 6 p.m., although there are several variations to the route. As at Neyland, there are no buses on Sundays. If you think that you might use this service, don't leave it to chance – get a timetable! Alternatively, you could always walk both ways as the distance involved is not particularly great.

Both of these walks are well served by pubs, Saundersfoot and Neyland being the most obvious places to look. Rosemarket, Johnston and Wiseman's Bridge all had one pub each when I visited, but the government's 'reforms' of the licensed trade have made life difficult for many publicans and it is a sad fact of life that many villages have now lost their local. We must hope that these three are not among them! The national giant Bass dominates the local scene, but Felinfoel and Crown Buckley (both from Llanelli) are also available.

6
THE SWANSEA BIKEPATH NETWORK

Gowerton to Black Pill and Swansea to Mumbles

Introduction

'Mumbles. Fairlie. Liverpool Crosby.' The walks in this chapter give you a chance to visit one of the places made famous by the BBC's 'Late Night Weather Report from Coastal Stations'. Mumbles turns out to be an attractive fishing village on the south-east corner of the Gower Peninsula, with a lighthouse perched on the second of two gaunt, rocky islands which jut out into Swansea Bay. The view across the bay reveals that this part of West Glamorgan has been developed extensively, from the tower blocks of Swansea to the vast expanse of Margam steel works.

Petrol, steel and chemicals are predominant in the area today, but in the past, Swansea was a vast workshop with a staggering range of industries. Coal and copper were pre-eminent, but many other products were extracted or manufactured locally: everything from iron, steel and zinc to sulphur, sulphuric acid and artificial manure. Add to this the fact that, by the 1880s, the town had become Britain's fifth largest ship-owning port and it is not difficult to see why railway companies flocked to Swansea like bees around a honey pot. The London & North Western, Midland and Great Western railways all had stations in the town, not to mention local companies such as the Rhondda & Swansea Bay and Swansea & Mumbles railways.

Needless to say, this level of competition has not survived and Swansea is now essentially a Great Western town with rail facilities concentrated on that company's old High Street terminus. Despite this, however, the old Swansea & Mumbles and London & North Western trackbeds can still be followed, thanks to the city's pioneering work in providing off-road cycle routes. On the other hand, the redevelopment of the foreshore has removed much of the distinctive railway character from these trails and it is only in the Clyne Valley (between Black Pill and Dunvant) that one is really aware of being on an old railway formation. Perhaps the best approach is to explore these lines by bicycle, for the extra speed eliminates any risk of monotony, and it must be said that the city council has installed a first class surface – good enough to entice even hardened walkers and motorists on to two wheels. Cycle hire facilities are available at Oystermouth.

History

A. Swansea Victoria to Pontardulais

The line from Swansea Victoria to Pontardulais was built by the Llanelly Railway, which was incorporated as the Llanelly Railroad & Dock Company on 19 June 1828. The LR&D was a vigorous concern with considerable territorial ambitions but its directors lacked judgement; for example, the high dividends paid to investors were financed partly by neglecting routine maintenance, as well as over-working the locomotives and rolling stock.

The Llanelly Railway was one of five companies involved in developing the modern Central Wales line: its contributions were the sections from Llanelly to Pontardulais (opened 1 June 1839) and Pontardulais to Llandilo (opened 24 January 1857). It also controlled the section from Llandilo to Llandovery via a lease of the separate Vale of Towy Railway. The long delay in reaching Llandilo was caused by the company's reckless management, which left the railway ill-equipped and financially weak. For example, by 1846, its four steam locomotives were in such poor condition that they had to be withdrawn for major repairs while the line reverted to horse power.

Despite these setbacks, the LR was determined to tap the lucrative traffic available at Swansea and introduced, via contractors, a through service from Swansea to Llandilo in 1853. Unfortunately, the only part of this route which was then served by rail was Pontardulais to Duffryn (modern Tirydail), which meant that passengers were obliged to make long connecting horse-bus journeys at each end. It is hardly surprisingly that this service was withdrawn two years later.

Undaunted, the LR obtained powers in 1861 to construct a new line from Pontardulais to a site near the South Dock in Swansea, together with a short branch from Gowerton to Penclawdd on the Gower Peninsula. It was openly supported in this by the London & North Western Railway, which was soon to become a major player in the Swansea area. Both of these lines opened to

A busy scene pre-1923 at Mumbles Road station on the Shrewsbury–Swansea line, with the LNWR permanent way gang at work. The practice of burying the sleepers with ballast, as seen here in the foreground, was later prohibited on the grounds that it made it impossible for local gangers to see defects in the timber. The station was situated just west of the A4067 at GR 619908; today, the buildings are gone and most of the site has been graded away

Swansea City Archives Office

goods and mineral traffic in January 1866, but the passenger openings were delayed until 14 December 1867 due mainly to the slowness of the builders at Swansea Victoria station. The main line was built initially as single track with intermediate stations at Pontardulais South (later Gorseinon), Gowerton (later Gowerton South), Dunvant, Killay and Mumbles Road. The LNWR opened further stations at Swansea Bay and Grovesend in 1878 and 1910 respectively.

In 1868, the LR's lease of the Vale of Towy Railway (Llandilo-Llandovery) came up for renewal. However, the LNWR had now reached Llandovery via its interests in the Central Wales and Central Wales Extension Railways, and was eager to gain access to Swansea and west Wales. By clever diplomacy, it persuaded the LR to make the new lease of the Vale of Towy Railway a joint one with itself, and also persuaded the local company to grant running powers over its lines to Swansea, Llanelly and Carmarthen. These were generous concessions by any measure and the LR soon realized the scale of its misjudgement. It challenged these clauses all the way to the House of Lords but failed totally to get them changed.

Penmaenpool on the former Cambrian Railways' branch from Barmouth Junction to Dolgellau is a good place to sample the old branch line atmosphere. The whole area has been sympathetically preserved, complete with signals, signal-box, station nameboard and attractive station house. There is also a rather fine hotel on site, which encourages casual visitors to linger!

Author

Although nothing more than a contractors' line, the Elan Valley Railway was extremely well built as the stonework on this bridge illustrates. The span and railings are modern additions installed by Welsh Water in the late 1980s, but prior to this, the original timbers still remained in place after nearly eighty years of abandonment – a tribute to the quality of the materials used

Author

The upshot of this action was very surprising: the LR's branches from Pontardulais to Swansea and Llandilo to Carmarthen were hived off into a separate company called the Swansea & Carmarthen Railway, while the LR itself was reduced to a minor concern with a mere 36 miles of track plus various running powers. This undermined its viability and it signed a lease to the GWR in 1873. In the same year, the Swansea & Carmarthen Railway sold the Swansea line and the connecting Penclawdd branch to the LNWR for £310,000. The LNWR now had what it wanted – direct access to Swansea – and various improvements followed. The most notable of these were the construction of a new terminus at Swansea Victoria in 1882 and the doubling of the whole line south of Pontardulais in 1892.

Following these early political manœuvres, the Swansea branch settled down to a relatively quiet life. The most notable event in its history was a visit by King Edward VII and Queen Alexandra on 20 July 1904. The royal couple arrived at Swansea Docks in the royal yacht, *Victoria and Albert*, and then travelled from Swansea Victoria to Builth Road en route to Rhayader, where they were due to open the Elan Valley Reservoirs for the City of Birmingham Water Board (see Chapter 4). While viewing new installations in the docks area, they used a specially furnished saloon coach as a rest and retiring room; this had been borrowed from the Swansea & Mumbles Railway and was originally a battery-powered vehicle, the result of an early experiment with electric traction.

In 1923, most of the Central Wales line – including the Swansea branch – went into the London, Midland & Scottish Railway, but the next ten years were a fallow period when early promise failed to materialize. The first closures occurred in the depressed 1930s, with the Penclawdd branch losing its passenger service on 5 January 1931 and Grovesend station closing to all traffic on 6 June 1932. World War II brought further economies and restrictions, with Victoria station suffering severe damage in February 1941 from German air raids over Swansea town centre and docks. This destroyed the glazing in the overall roof, which neither the LMS nor its successors could afford to repair. The whole sorry period brought to the line an atmosphere of neglect and decay from which it never fully recovered.

With nationalization in 1948, the whole of the Central Wales line was transferred to the Western Region of the newly formed British Railways, but the process of decline continued as before with many branches suffering partial or complete closure. Each closure further reduced the need for locomotives and, as a result, BR closed Swansea's Paxton Street Motive Power Depot on 31 August 1959. In 1960, there was a brief period of optimism when plans were announced to develop the line as an important cross-country link, but then the policy was reconsidered and the scheme withdrawn.

The Western Region submitted its first definite closure proposals in June 1962, claiming that £202,000 per annum would be saved if the passenger service between Swansea and Shrewsbury was totally withdrawn. A public enquiry was held in Swansea in November that year, when the local Transport Users' Consultative Committee concluded that closure would cause hardship only to users between Craven Arms and Llandilo. This verdict doomed the Swansea branch to extinction, but it did at least save the rest of the line. The final scheme approved by the Minister of Transport was to keep the line open between Craven Arms and Pontardulais, but to close the branch from Pontardulais to Swansea due to the availability of other forms of public transport. In future, Central Wales trains would reach Swansea by continuing to Llanelli, where they would reverse on to the South Wales main line.

The section from Swansea Victoria to Pontardulais duly closed to passengers on Saturday 13 June 1964. The sombre mood was exacerbated by a notice outside the booking office at Victoria station which read, 'Did you use this line? – No? Why come now then? – it's too late!' The last train out was the 6.25 p.m. to Shrewsbury and York, while the last train in was the 6.00 p.m. from Shrewsbury which arrived shortly after 10.30 p.m. Goods services between Swansea Victoria and Gorseinon were withdrawn on 4 October 1965. Freight services between Pontardulais and Gorseinon survived in a piecemeal fashion until the 1980s, although the first mile south of Pontardulais was closed in 1974 when a new connection was opened from the GWR Swansea Avoiding Line to Grovesend. This enabled trains to reach Grovesend and Gorseinon, as before, but via a more roundabout route. Services between Grovesend and Gorseinon ceased in 1984, with the last stub north of Grovesend following in 1986.

Victoria station was demolished in 1966, by which time sand dunes had formed over the rails leading in from Swansea Bay. In the event, trains over the Central Wales line never reversed at Llanelli but terminated there instead; the Western Region decided that it was easier and cheaper to provide connections rather than through trains to Swansea.

B. Swansea (Rutland Street) to Mumbles

The Swansea & Mumbles Railway is a small company with a big history. Despite being a railway, its origins lie in the canal age. By 1798, Swansea had the benefit of two successful canals: the Tennant Canal from Port Tennant to Aberdulais, and the Swansea Canal from Swansea to Abercrave. In 1803, it was proposed to link Mumbles to this network via a cut along the coast with a branch up the Clyne Valley to serve local collieries. However, there was considerable opposition to this scheme, especially from the Swansea Canal which feared loss of water to the new branch, and the Swansea Harbour Trust which feared that the proposed basin at Mumbles might develop into a harbour to rival its own. As a result, the Act of 1804 authorized a tramway which was to be known as the Oystermouth Railway.

The goods yard outside Swansea Victoria, seen here some time before World War I, makes it obvious where the railway obtained most of its trade and profit. The private owners' wagons provide a wealth of colliery names from all over South Wales: Park and Blaina, North, Hedley, Davie, Loughor and S. Llewellyn are all evident in this photograph. Victoria Station was demolished in 1966 and this area has been redeveloped beyond all recognition

Swansea City Archives Office

Edward Martin, one of the promoters, had the foresight to include a clause allowing haulage by 'men, horses or otherwise', which paved the way for steam traction in years to come; he had read of Trevithick's pioneering run on the Pennydarren Tramway in the pages of *The Cambrian* newspaper.

By 1 September 1804, construction work had already started, the line being built with L-shaped tram plates mounted on stone blocks. Goods traffic was running by April 1806 and, on 25 March 1807, the line secured its place in history by becoming the first to carry fare-paying passengers. Despite this, all was not well financially and the company borrowed £1,500 on mortgage in 1808. Four years later, it was so far in arrears with its repayments that the mortgagor took possession, setting off a series of legal claims and counter claims which make the affairs of this small local concern among the most complex in British railway history.

Space does not permit a detailed explanation of these convoluted wranglings, except to say that the Morris family controlled the railway until the 1870s. In 1865, George Byng Morris sold the lease to John Dickson, a local railway contractor, but assumed that the sale was null and void when Dickson petitioned for bankruptcy a few years later. Morris then sold the lease to the Swansea Improvements & Tramways Company in 1877, only to have Dickson successfully contest this sale in the courts. Dickson also established that the tramway company was not authorized to run steam trains on the line, so between 1878 and 1885, and again between 1892 and 1896, he and his successors provided the steam services while the tramway company trundled along behind with a horse-drawn tram. The two protagonists slogged it out in the courts until Dickson's death in 1892, after which the tramway company gradually gained control.

While all this was going on, the line had a very chequered history. In 1838, storms swept away sections of the permanent way and, by 1840, the original line along the shore at Black Pill was abandoned and a road laid along its course. Further storms in 1846 compounded the damage. The tramway was still shown on maps and may have enjoyed some residual freight traffic, but it was in a very run-down state and passenger services had ceased altogether. George Byng Morris began the revival by replacing the L-shaped tram plates with ordinary rails between 1855 and 1860. The new track enabled him to reintroduce passenger services between Swansea and Black Pill in August 1860, with an extension to Oystermouth following five months later. By 1865, there were eight trains in each direction per weekday, taking 43 minutes for the 5 mile journey.

Morris's new service lasted for seventeen years, by which time it had become an anachronism – not least because the company was still using horse-drawn trains at a time when steam railways had become commonplace. It is hardly surprising, then, that on 16 August 1877 the Swansea Improvements & Tramways Company (the putative leaseholder of the line) carried out a successful trial with the steam locomotive *Pioneer*. Due to the legal wrangles with John Dickson, it was he who introduced regular steam services over the line in 1878, and these then became the norm until 1929. Motive power was supplied by 0–4–0 or 0–6–0 side or saddle tanks, which had no difficulty in achieving the modest speeds required on the largely level track.

The next milestone in the company's history was an Act of 1889 which authorized the construction of Mumbles Pier and the extension of the railway to meet it. Work commenced in 1892 and, on 6 May 1893, passenger services were inaugurated between Oystermouth and Southend. Later that year, the line became known as the Swansea & Mumbles Railway following the enactment of a bill on 26 July. Mumbles Pier and the railway link from Southend were opened five years later on 10 May 1898. From the outset, the new pier became a very popular attraction and remained so until the onset of World War I. It also became the starting place for White Funnel steamer excursions to Ilfracombe, Weston-super-Mare and Lynmouth, as well as local trips along the Gower coast.

On 1 July 1899, the Swansea Improvements & Tramways Company (now owned by British Electric Traction) took on a 999 year lease of the line. BET introduced electric trams in Swansea the following year, but the cost of electrifying the Mumbles line was considered prohibitive, so two battery-powered 'accumulator cars' were bought instead in 1902. Unfortunately, these proved unsuccessful in trials and from 1903 were used as ordinary steam-hauled rolling stock. In 1927, the tramways company merged with the South Wales Transport Company, which immediately set about electrifying the old line. By January 1928, a new electricity substation had been completed at Black Pill (fed by a supply from the municipal power station in The Strand), while the track was relaid with 85 lb rails, new ballast and many new sleepers. A proper signalling system was also installed, together with extra passing loops. The catenary poles started going up in February 1928, while the first overhead wires were hung four months later. Finally, 13 new double-decker electric tramcars were delivered, each having a seating capacity of 106. Locals at the time were pleased to see that their upper decks were enclosed, unlike their steam-hauled predecessors!

The new electric service was inaugurated on 2 March 1929 with the 4.30 a.m. departure from the company's Rutland Street terminus. The renewal of the system cost £125,000, but the investment paid handsome dividends in terms of increased passenger traffic: in 1925, the steam trains conveyed 682,108 passengers, but this figure exceeded 1 million in 1938 and was approaching 5 million in 1945. Even after World War II, the electric trams continued to hold their own, with over three million passengers using them in 1953.

The following year, the 150th anniversary of the line was celebrated in style with replica steam and horse trains joining a grand parade. Unfortunately, by this time the Swansea & Mumbles was again an anachronism, for trams elsewhere in Swansea had been withdrawn in 1936. Many towns in the 1930s had come to regard trams as obsolete, and there was the added worry that the South Wales Transport Company – the railway's ultimate owner – was primarily a bus company. It is not surprising that the decision to close the line was taken shortly afterwards in 1958. Passenger numbers were declining and the cost of maintaining, let alone renewing, the system was rising. The mood of the time favoured roads, and this is ultimately what killed the line.

SWT bought the remaining lease in September 1958 and, two months later, presented a bill for the railway's closure to Parliament. This was duly passed in July 1959. As a result, the section from Southend to Mumbles Pier closed on 11 October 1959, with the section from Swansea to Southend following on 5 January 1960. Demolition began immediately afterwards, although a short freight-only section east of Rutland Street survived until 1962. (This had been leased to the Swansea Harbour Trust in 1897, passing thence to the Great Western Railway in 1923 and British Railways Western Region in 1948.) One of the electric tramcars was removed to the Middleton Railway for restoration, but was vandalized a few years later. The front end of tramcar No. 7, on display in Swansea Maritime and Industrial Museum, is a replica built for the line's 175th anniversary celebrations.

This photograph from *c.* 1964 depicts Killay station in the Clyne Valley – just after passenger services were withdrawn, to judge by the vegetation encroaching on the platform. Despite the main line status of the Shrewsbury–Swansea route, its course through the valley was very sinuous, as made evident here. The station buildings have long since gone but parts of the platforms remain, together with the Railway Inn (the two-storey building by the bridge), which now serves the needs of walkers and cyclists rather than intending passengers

Swansea City Archives Office

The Lines Today

After closure, Swansea City Council acquired both lines within its boundaries and converted them for leisure and recreation use. The demise of the two railways enabled a conventional promenade to be created along Swansea Bay, and nowadays few holidaymakers realize that a stroll along the sea front is actually a railway ramble. The Swansea Bikepath Network was established in the 1980s and currently runs from Swansea Maritime Quarter to Mumbles, with a spur up the Clyne Valley to Gowerton. Further developments are in progress, the most notable being a new path up the Tawe Valley to Morriston and Clydach, where the towpath of the Swansea Canal has already been upgraded. This can be followed northwards as far as Ynysmeudwy (about two miles south of Ystalyfera).

The old LNWR line to Pontardulais is owned by Swansea City Council as far as Dunvant, after which ownership passes to Lliw Valley Borough Council. This authority has already extended the bikepath from Dunvant to Gowerton and is currently working on a further extension to Grovesend. In August 1993, one and a half miles between Gorseinon and Grovesend were already complete, and the link between Gowerton and Gorseinon was scheduled to be in place by April 1994.

Finally, Swansea City Council intends to contribute to a long distance cycle trail from Swansea to Newport. The existing bikepath will form part of this route, but an eastern extension is planned from the Maritime Quarter to the city boundary at Crymlyn Marsh, where it will meet a cycle trail being developed from Neath. This could follow the course of the old GWR line to Jersey Marine, although it is more likely to use the towpath of the adjoining Tennant Canal.

Walk 1 – Gowerton to Black Pill (4 miles)

The LNWR station at Gowerton stood at GR 592962, just south of the B4295. It was renamed Gowerton South by British Railways in January 1950 to avoid confusion with the nearby ex-GWR station, which remains open to this day. There was a level crossing just north of the station, followed immediately by Gowerton Junction which gave access to the single track branch to Penclawdd and Llanmorlais. A hundred yards later, the main line crossed the GWR Swansea–Llanelly railway by a bridge which has long been demolished. The site of the junction now accommodates a large car park, but the trackbed can be discerned at the north end disappearing into some bushes.

Gowerton station site survives as a large, grassed area bounded on the south by a pair of brick walls which stand marooned in the middle of the trackbed. Beyond these, the line is obstructed by garden extensions so it is necessary to follow the B4296 to the southern edge of the town in order to pick up the bikepath to Swansea. The cycle trail begins at GR 595952 where the old railway is crossed by a bridleway, conveniently signposted from the road. Follow the bridleway to the site of a demolished bridge, then turn right and climb the bank to reach the start.

The trail begins on an embankment but soon enters a cutting, which it follows for a mile to Dunvant station. The cutting is flanked by deciduous trees and a drainage channel on the left, which runs a vivid, rust-red colour suggesting the presence of metal ore deposits nearby. In places, the rock strata through which the line was cut are still exposed; they now support a

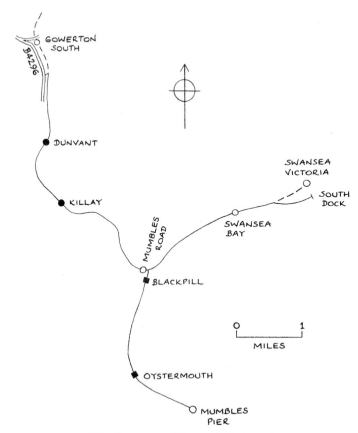

The Swansea Bikepath Network

variety of mosses and ferns which have found a toehold in the cracks and crevices. As I cycled up the bank (a gentle gradient of 1 in 72), I startled a green woodpecker which flew off ahead of me, its characteristic yelping cry echoing through the surrounding woods. Before the cycle trail was constructed, this section of the line was impassable due to flooding and dense vegetation, so the local authority must be complimented on the thoroughness of its restoration work.

Dunvant station stood at the summit of the line at GR 594938. Two empty platforms survive along with a pair of semi-detached railway houses, but there appears to be no trace of the timber booking office and waiting-rooms. But look carefully: the white-painted shed by the house on the left used to be the waiting-room on the Up platform. Immediately south of the station, the line passes under the B4296 before negotiating a long curve to the left which takes it over the infant Clyne River at GR 592932. The

Part of a medieval fortification, perhaps, or the ancient town walls of Swansea? No: this is part of the stone-faced embankment that carried trains of the London & North Western Railway into Swansea Victoria. It now forms the northern boundary of Swansea Maritime Quarter, formerly the town's South Dock

Author

gradient then steepens to 1 in 70 as it approaches Killay, which is preceded by a choice of routes; take the trail on the right.

Killay station was situated at GR 598923, just south of a bridge carrying the A4118 over the line. Only the platforms remain today. The fact that they appear to be barely inches tall reveals that this part of the trackbed was used as a landfill site for some years. The other notable thing about Killay station is the survival of the adjoining Railway Inn, which has recently escaped from the clutches of a national brewer and now serves the full range of Crown Buckley beers. It's an unusual pub, full of character, being built into the side of the railway cutting. The lounge bar contains some interesting memorabilia, including a large map which reveals the size of the rail network before Dr Beeching and his successors started pruning it.

South of Killay, the trail enters the wooded Clyne Valley which has now been developed as a country park. Swansea City Council purchased the 220 acres of Clyne Woods in 1980 and has been improving the area ever since. The park includes a wide variety of natural habitats – everything from steep gorges to abandoned industrial workings – which support a great diversity of plants, animals and birds. The converted railway line is the 'spine path' and has several other trails connecting with it. Perhaps the most striking feature en route is the lake at GR 613913. The water-lilies here, and the overhanging trees with their gnarled and twisted roots, are reminiscent of an illustration by Arthur Rackham. This idyllic scene used to be completely overgrown and hidden; nowadays, it is one of the park's showpieces.

Just south of the lake, a narrow lane will be seen curving in on the left. The width and gradient of this suggest a railway origin and it turns out to be part of the Clyne Valley branch of the Swansea & Mumbles Railway. This was constructed in 1804 to serve quarries in the area but closed early in the twentieth century when they became uneconomical to work. The site of Mumbles Road station follows soon after at GR 619908. There are no discernible remains of this windswept halt because the embankment on which it stood has been graded away. The only feature there today, a small paved area with some seating, is entirely modern.

Immediately beyond Mumbles Road station, the railway crossed the Swansea–Mumbles highway by Black Pill Bridge. This was followed by a very tight curve to the left which often dislodged coal from passing trains; it used to spill out of open wagons and engine bunkers on to the embankment, to be gathered up by scouts and others camping near Clyne Woods. Very little of this remains today, although as you stand on the site of Mumbles Road station, you can see the remains of the railway embankment on the far side of the A4067. Take care when you cross this road, as it is very busy. The rest of the line to Swansea Victoria survives as part of the cycle trail along the promenade and is described in the next section.

Walk 2 – Swansea to Mumbles (5 miles)

The LNWR line to Shrewsbury and the tramway to Mumbles both started from the north side of Swansea South Dock (GR 657924). The LNWR's Victoria station was an unprepossessing affair at GR 658927 with a flimsy-looking overall roof, the glazing of which was destroyed by enemy action during World War II (see above); the site is now occupied by the leisure centre in Oystermouth Road. The Rutland Street terminus of the Swansea & Mumbles Railway stood immediately west of Victoria station and was another piece of uninspired architecture, looking rather like an outbuilding from a 1930s secondary school.

The whole of this area has been redeveloped and it is worth spending some time here. The South Dock is now a yachting marina and many of the old warehouses have been demolished to make way for new housing. One warehouse which did survive is Wind Street Goods Station, which now forms

Oystermouth station on the Swansea & Mumbles Railway now serves as the local Tourist Information Centre. The adjoining waiting shelter has been demolished, but a tram pole at the far end of the building survives in adapted form as a street light. The site is now owned by South Wales Transport, the local bus operator, which has been threatening to redevelop the site for years

David James Photography (Sussex)

part of the Swansea Maritime and Industrial Museum. The tramshed annexe next door houses the remains of the Swansea & Mumbles Railway (including a replica front end of tramcar No. 7), while a number of large floating exhibits are berthed in the dock outside. These include a lightship, a steam tug and a lifeboat; the nearby galleon turns out to be a floating pub and restaurant. Behind all this runs a long stone-faced embankment which once carried the LNWR main line and a GWR link to High Street Junction, just north of the present BR terminus. Similar stonework occurs in places all along the modern promenade and is one of the few signs that it is, in fact, an old railway formation.

The modern bikepath starts on the sea wall, so it is necessary to cross the footbridge by the restored pump house and head for the shore. It is only a hundred yards or so and there are several paths and passageways to choose from. Once on the sea wall, turn right, passing the new housing built around the marina; this replaces two large warehouses and a network of sidings built to serve them. Immediately beyond lay Paxton Street Motive Power Depot, which included yet more sidings, a six-road engine shed and a turntable; all of this has been replaced by a modern hotel and the grey slabs of West Glamorgan County Hall.

Beyond County Hall, the trail curves in to join the main coast road which it follows fairly closely all the way to Mumbles. Originally, the LNWR ran along the sea wall with the Swansea & Mumbles Railway alongside, but the dualling of the road here has removed almost every trace of both lines. Nothing remains of the SMR station at St Helens (GR 644922), although a massive girder bridge, which crossed the road and all three running lines, remains in place a short distance beyond. The LNWR's Swansea Bay station, a windswept timber affair at GR 641921, has vanished without trace.

The next station on the SMR was Brynmill (GR 636919), which stood near the modern university. By this stage, the course of both lines is clearly evident, with the LNWR forming the modern promenade and the SMR a tarmacked strip a few yards inland. The cycle trail is now following the SMR but soon switches to the LNWR, which it then follows all the way to Black Pill. This section does actually resemble an old railway, for the trail is flanked on both sides by straggly hedges and, like the railway before it, suffers from sand blowing on to the permanent way. The course of the SMR has disappeared beneath an adjoining golf course.

What is a railway bridge doing in the middle of the busy A4067 along Swansea seafront? Answer: in 1960 the road was single rather than dual carriageway, and was accompanied by no less than three railway lines – the single track Swansea & Mumbles Railway, and the double track Swansea–Shrewsbury line of the LNWR. The railway built the bridge to allow bathers to reach the seafront in safety

David James Photography (Sussex)

At Black Pill, the trail curves right on the approach to the now demolished Black Pill Bridge; if you are heading for Gowerton, follow this to the main road, cross over and continue up the Clyne Valley. However, if you are heading for Mumbles, turn left on to a narrower trail which leads down the embankment and crosses the Clyne river by a modern concrete bridge. You will then be on the course of the Swansea & Mumbles Railway, which can be followed all the way to Mumbles Pier.

The next feature of note is Black Pill station (GR 619906), which also served as an electricity substation. This is the principal relic of the railway and survives completely intact. It is an elegant building with some classical touches, such as the rounded windows and the colonnaded platform for waiting passengers. The roof is crowned with a large stone bearing the station name and, when I visited, a series of panels on the platform gave a brief account of the line's history.

South of Black Pill, the line becomes very leafy and genteel, and there is some rare evidence of engineering work where several courses of facing stones line the right-hand side of a shallow cutting. Nothing remains of West Cross station (GR 615888), but Oystermouth station (GR 617882) survives as a Tourist Information Office in the midst of the local bus depot. The bus company, South Wales Transport, has been threatening to redevelop this site for years, but nothing so far has come of it. Beyond Oystermouth, the trackbed is lined with boats – as it always was – but these are now pleasure rather than fishing craft.

Southend station (GR 624877), like so many of the others, survives only as a memory. It was situated near the modern glass-built café, whose design recalls the Victorian pavilion which once stood on Mumbles Pier. The approach road to the pier itself is built directly on the old trackbed. It is only some 600 yd long but still features the masts which held the overhead electric wires; these have found a new purpose in life as street lights. The Pier Hotel, once a popular haunt with visitors waiting for the Swansea train, still does a good trade but beyond this civilization comes to an end: nothing lies ahead but two rocky, grass-flecked islands, the furthest surmounted by Mumbles Head Lighthouse. An official sign warns 'Do not walk to the island: fast rising tide'. It does not look the sort of place where one would wish to be marooned.

Further Explorations

Given the rich industrial heritage of the Swansea area, many old canal and railway routes can still be traced on the ground. Mention has already been made of the towpath of the Swansea Canal, which can be walked from

Clydach to Ynysmeudwy (4 miles), while the towpath of the Tennant Canal can be followed to Neath across the industrial landscape of Crymlyn Marsh. If you wish to see an operational canal, it is necessary to travel a few miles beyond Neath to Resolven, where a 4 mile section of the Neath Canal has been restored, including 7 locks, 2 aqueducts, 4 bridges and 2 canal basins. (Not all of these towpaths are public rights of way, so sections may be closed occasionally by the canal company, especially when repairs are necessary.)

On the railway side, the gap in the Clyne Valley route between Gowerton and Gorseinon should be filled in the next few years, while an extension to Pontardulais is a long term possibility. A cycle trail has also been established in Penclawdd along a ½ mile section of the former line from Gowerton to Llanmorlais. (Other sections of this branch can be traced from the B4295, which accompanies the railway for nearly its whole length.) To the north-east of Swansea, Lliw Valley Borough Council plans to build a railway path from Pontardawe to Ystalyfera (4 miles), which is programmed for completion by April 1994. Finally, the Swansea Vale Railway is rebuilding a 1½ mile section of the old Midland line between Six Pit Junction (GR 680968) and Upper Bank station.

Transport and Facilities

Maps: Ordnance Survey: Landranger Series Sheet 159

Buses: South Wales Transport, Quadrant Bus Station,
               1 Plymouth Street, Swansea, SA1 3QF
               Telephone: Swansea (0792) 475511

               West Glamorgan County Council, Environment & Highways,
               County Hall, Swansea, SA1 3SN
               Telephone: Swansea (0792) 471127 (direct line)

               South Wales Transport is the major operator in the Swansea area, but a few smaller companies also provide useful services. Details of these can be obtained from West Glamorgan County Council.

Trains: British Rail Telephone Enquiry Bureau
               Telephone: Swansea (0792) 467777

Swansea Vale Railway, Six Pit Junction,
Nant-y-Ffin Road, Llansamlet, Swansea
Telephone: Swansea (0792) 467045

Cycle Hire: Swansea Bay Cycle Hire, Village Lane, Boat Park,
Mumbles, nr. Swansea (Easter to September only)
Telephone: Swansea (0792) 814290 or 818248

Hire charges are £1.75 per hour for a standard bike or £2.00 per hour for a mountain bike, with reductions for longer hire periods (1994).

The bus services in Swansea are excellent and there is little need for visitors to plan a day's walking around the bus timetable. The minibus service from Swansea Quadrant Bus Station to Oystermouth is particularly good, with a bus every five minutes on weekdays and every half hour on Sundays. The service to Killay is equally good, although there are only weekday buses to Dunvant and Gowerton: four per hour to Dunvant, and two per hour to Gowerton. Only walkers aiming for Grovesend need to plan their journey, for the service here is sparse indeed. It consists of two early morning trips into Swansea, and three early evening trips the other way. This problem can be eliminated, of course, by hiring a bicycle and riding both ways.

As for refreshments, there are no practical difficulties as most of the bikepath network is in an urban area with shops, pubs and cafés always close at hand. My favourite stop is the Railway Inn at Killay, but there are plenty of other pubs to choose from. If in doubt, go for one of the independent local brewers: Brains, Felinfoel or Crown Buckley.

7
THE AFAN VALLEY

Afan Argoed Country Park

Introduction

The Afan Valley runs north-east from Port Talbot for approximately 11 miles to the remote village of Blaengwynfi, where the vast bulk of Mynydd Blaengwynfi provides a dramatic barrier between the Afan and Rhondda valleys. Sparsely populated by a tight-knit community of sheep farmers, the area was transformed in the nineteenth century by the commercial exploitation of local iron and coal reserves. The first railway arrived in 1861 and, by the turn of the century, the valley had become highly industrialized – a transformation achieved with some difficulty to judge by contemporary tales of pitched battles with Irish navvies.

Nowadays industry has gone, and extensive landscaping has restored the Afan Valley to its former glory. Afan Argoed Country Park occupies 3,000 of the valley's 35,000 acres and is one of the major recreational facilities in West Glamorgan. It includes a new £350,000 countryside centre, the award-winning South Wales Miners' Museum, over 30 miles of waymarked circular walks and a veritable feast for railway ramblers – 14 miles of cycle trails built on abandoned trackbeds. The industrial heritage here is very rich, as revealed by the fact that no less than nine separate companies were involved in providing the valley's network of tramways and railways. Even the valley road, the A4107, is laid for part of its length along the course of the Oakwood Tramway, an early line constructed in the 1750s with wooden rails. Its most notable relic is Bont Fawr Aqueduct at Pontrhydyfen, built in the 1820s as a tramway bridge but later used for water supply; it has now been tarmacked over and is used as a local road.

History

A. Gyfylchi Tunnel to Cymmer and Glyncorrwg
Disregarding the early tramways, the first proper railway to enter the Afan Valley was the South Wales Mineral Railway, a broad gauge line whose engineer was no less than the renowned Isambard Kingdom Brunel. The company was promoted by prospective colliery owners in the upper Afan Valley who wanted to establish an efficient link with the nearest sea port, Briton Ferry. Brunel surveyed a very direct route for them, but unfortunately it included a 1,109 yd tunnel at Gyfylchi and a 1½ mile incline at Ynys-y-Maerdy, near the western terminus. These engineering features were to cost the company, both in terms of construction and subsequent operating costs. Another problem was the company's dependence on a

This turn-of-the-century view of Glyncorrwg is not that different to what one sees today, although the railway in the foreground is now but an empty track. Note the row of loaded wagons from the Glyncorrwg Colliery Company awaiting shipment to Cymmer and beyond, and the bare mountains in the background. The railway continued another 2 miles up the valley of the Afon Corrwg past North Rhondda Halt, where miners alighted for their daily work at Glyncorrwg North and South Pits

West Glamorgan County Council

single source of traffic, i.e. coal from Glyncorrwg, and its vulnerability if that traffic failed.

Oblivious to these problems, the promoters pressed ahead. The South Wales Mineral Railway was duly authorized on 15 August 1853 and opened its line from Briton Ferry to the western end of Gyfylchi Tunnel on 1 September 1861. It opened the remaining 6 miles to Glyncorrwg eighteen months later on 10 March 1863. During this period, the Glyncorrwg Coal Company signed a 30 year lease on the line and, in 1870, took over day-to-day operations of the railway. By now, the fortunes of the two companies were so intertwined that, when the coal company went bankrupt in 1878, the railway soon followed suit. The reasons for the disaster were not hard to see: a slump in the mining industry; the impoverished state of the railway after its long period of construction; and the recent expense of converting the line to standard gauge – a switch necessitated by the GWR's abandonment of the broad gauge on its South Wales main line in 1872.

The SWMR secretary, T.J. Woods, was appointed receiver and kept the railway going until 1880 when it was leased by the new Glyncorrwg Colliery Company (note the subtle change of name). The colliery company was established to take over the business of the old coal company, but both it and the railway continued to be unprosperous: while the one over-estimated the growth of coal traffic, the other was burdened with the high operating costs of Ynys-y-Maerdy Incline. To add insult to injury, when the coal traffic finally did increase, the incline acted as a bottleneck that prevented further expansion. Relief finally came from the Port Talbot Railway, which made a connection at the western end of Gyfylchi Tunnel on 14 November 1898. This provided the SWMR with an alternative outlet to the modern harbour at Port Talbot. Given the mineral railway's need to avoid the incline, it is not surprising that the two railways remained on friendly terms. This culminated in an agreement whereby the SWMR was to be worked by the PTR from 30 March 1908. As the latter had already made a similar arrangement with the GWR, the mineral railway was actually worked by the Great Western Railway on and from this date.

The advent of the GWR finally heralded a period of modest prosperity, which included the introduction of passenger services between Cymmer and Glyncorrwg. These started on 28 March 1918 and lasted until 22 September 1930, although unadvertised colliers' trains continued until 2 November 1964. In the mid-1950s these services used ex-GWR Dean clerestory four-wheel coaches, which made them unique as the last bastion of this antique stock.

The line closed in stages with the incline at Ynys-y-Maerdy going first in 1910. The next major closure occurred on 13 July 1947 when part of Gyfylchi Tunnel collapsed, leading to the withdrawal of services between it and Abercregan (near Cymmer). Thereafter the line was worked in two halves, with the ex-PTR line giving access to the section west of the tunnel, and an 1878 link at Cymmer giving access to the steeply graded Glyncorrwg line. The rest of the system closed with the local collieries. The section from Cymmer to Abercregan went on 1 May 1961; the section west of Gyfylchi Tunnel on 2 November 1964; and the final link from Cymmer to Glyncorrwg on 24 August 1970.

B. Cymmer to Abergwynfi

The second line to enter the Afan Valley was built by the Llynfi & Ogmore Railway, although services were always operated by the GWR. The story of this line starts with the Llynfi Valley Railway, which was incorporated on 7 August 1846 and opened a branch line from Bridgend to Nantyffyllon on 10 August 1861. Amalgamation with the neighbouring Ogmore Valley Railway in 1866 formed the Llynfi & Ogmore Railway, and it was this joint company which obtained powers in July 1873 to build an extension from Nantyffyllon to Abergwynfi at the head of the Afan Valley. The same Act also confirmed an agreement with the GWR, whereby the larger company was to work and manage the L&OR from 1 July 1876.

No through road! Would-be tunnel explorers are advised to steer well clear of the 1109 yd Gyfylchi Tunnel on the former South Wales Mineral Railway, which once linked the Afan and Pellena valleys. The west end of the tunnel collapsed on 13 July 1947 and the bore is now waterlogged to a depth of over 3 ft. In this scene, a group of enthusiasts inspect the damage on 29 May 1954. Note that the rails are still in place, seven years after the event

D.K. Jones

The extension to Abergwynfi involved a 1,594 yd tunnel south of Cymmer, which was bored between 1875 and 1877. The new route opened throughout on 1 July 1878, together with a link to the SWMR at Cymmer. This ran from the south to the north side of the Afan Valley via an elegant lattice girder bridge which stands to this day. The company had originally intended to build a stone viaduct here with nine 40 ft spans, but had to adapt its plans due to a shortage of stonemasons. The new link provided an alternative outlet for Glyncorrwg coal, but did not open soon enough to prevent the bankruptcy of the SWMR and its parent company. Fortunately, the new line had another important source of traffic, namely the Western (later Avon) Colliery at Abergwynfi, which was sunk in 1877 by Sir Daniel Gooch and others as a source of high quality locomotive coal for the GWR. This pit remained open until September 1969 and was instrumental in sustaining the line long after it might otherwise have closed. Passenger services from Nantyffyllon commenced on 16 July 1880 but initially ran as far as Cymmer only; they were extended to Abergwynfi on 22 March 1886.

The closure of this line was relatively complicated. The section from Cymmer to Abergwynfi closed officially to passengers on 13 June 1960, but a service was still available via the parallel ex-Rhondda & Swansea Bay line. This linked Cymmer and Blaengwynfi, whose station was less than half a mile from the ex-GWR Abergwynfi. The irony is that on the same day, British Railways closed the ex-Rhondda & Swansea Bay line between Cymmer and Blaengwynfi and routed all services over the GWR Abergwynfi branch via new connecting spurs at each end. Thus a rail journey from Swansea to Treherbert still used the top end of the Abergwynfi branch although, for official purposes, it had closed.

On 3 December 1962, the ex-R&SBR services from Swansea to Treherbert were withdrawn, but new services from Bridgend to Treherbert were introduced at the same time. These continued until 26 February 1968, when serious earth movement was detected in the Rhondda Tunnel between Blaengwynfi and Treherbert. This effectively finished services east of Cymmer. Rhondda Tunnel was closed temporarily for repairs but never reopened. Trains continued to run between Cymmer and Bridgend until 22 June 1970, but then they too were withdrawn. The very last passenger trains were special school services between Cymmer and Llangynwyd; these operated until 15 July 1970.

Freight services disappeared more or less simultaneously. They were withdrawn between Cymmer and Abergwynfi on 27 May 1963, and between Cymmer and Caerau on 24 August 1970. (This last closure was, of course, part of the general withdrawal from Glyncorrwg.) The final train to leave Cymmer was the demolition train, which departed with a load of recovered rails on 22 May 1971.

C. Pontrhydyfen to Cymmer and Blaengwynfi

The third line to reach the area was built by the Rhondda & Swansea Bay Railway, which was unusual in using the whole length of the Afan Valley. The R&SBR was supported principally by colliery owners at the top end of the Rhondda Valley and shipping interests in Swansea. The colliery owners were frustrated by congestion on the Taff Vale Railway, which delayed transport of their coal to the docks at Cardiff and Penarth, while the rival GWR service to Swansea sometimes had wagons in transit for over a week. The R&SBR proposed a new line from the Rhondda to Swansea, which would solve both of these problems at once.

The company received its Act on 10 August 1882. It is interesting to note that, in its original form, the scheme suffered from the same problem as the South Wales Mineral Railway, namely an obsession with following the shortest possible route regardless of geographical and engineering considerations. To this end, the company originally planned to build a long tunnel from Baglan to Pontrhydyfen, with a branch running down the Afan Valley to serve Port Talbot. Oddly enough, the GWR – then implacably opposed to the R&SBR reaching Swansea by its own metals – was instrumental in bringing the newcomer to its senses.

In order to reach Swansea the R&SBR would have to cross the River Neath just below the town, but local shipping interests were concerned that this would hinder their trade. The GWR orchestrated this opposition so effectively that the R&SBR's Act was modified to authorize a line from Treherbert to Briton Ferry only. When the GWR offered a traffic agreement using the South Wales main line between Port Talbot and Swansea, the R&SBR decided to abandon the Baglan Tunnel and head straight down the Afan Valley instead. Then the GWR over-played its hand. In an attempt to strangle its rival, it proposed hopelessly inadequate junction arrangements at Port Talbot. This sent the R&SBR scurrying back to Parliament for powers to construct an independent line to Swansea, which were duly granted in 1892.

The line was built in stages with the section from Aberavon to Cymmer opening first on 2 November 1885. An extension from Cymmer to Blaengwynfi followed on 2 June 1890 and, exactly a month later, R&SBR trains reached Blaenrhondda on the east side of the 3,443 yd Rhondda Tunnel – the longest to be constructed entirely in South Wales. Treherbert was reached on 14 July 1890, after which the company set its sights on Swansea. Danygraig was reached on 14 December 1894, with the final mile to Swansea (Riverside) opening on 7 May 1899.

The profits of the R&SBR were initially lean but picked up as the Welsh coalfield expanded. Even the hostility of the GWR dissolved when, in 1902, the Barry Railway was given powers to invest in a new Neath, Pontardawe and Brynamman Railway which proposed to link various GWR lines with those of rivals such as the Midland Railway and the R&SBR. Faced with the extension of Barry influence from Cardiff to Swansea, the GWR made friendly overtures to the Rhondda company and proposed a lease, which guaranteed dividends the like of which its shareholders had never seen. Under the circumstances, the directors recommended acceptance of the GWR's terms, and the lease took effect from 1 July 1906.

Following the GWR take-over, services continued fairly much as before although three new GWR locomotives were supplied to work the passenger trains. In 1936, passenger services at the Swansea end were rationalized when Briton Ferry station was rebuilt, allowing Treherbert trains to reach the GWR terminus at Swansea High Street; thereafter, the R&SBR route to Swansea (Riverside) was used for goods only. The main closures, as so often happened, came in the 1960s. On 13 June 1960, British Railways created a 'composite' route from Swansea to Treherbert by diverting R&SBR services on to the ex-GWR Abergwynfi branch between Cymmer and Blaengwynfi. The rest of the story has been told in the previous section, certainly as far as closure of the Rhondda Tunnel on 26 February 1968. By this time, passenger services to Treherbert ran from Bridgend rather than Swansea, but closure of the tunnel was intended, initially at least, to be temporary rather than permanent. To this end, BR introduced a replacement bus service between Cymmer and Treherbert which connected with trains at both ends – after a fashion. To describe this service as execrable is being generous. Trains from Cymmer to Treherbert took nineteen minutes; the replacement bus took one hour. The service between Cymmer and Blaenrhondda was even worse. To add insult to injury, the connection times at Treherbert were rarely less than thirty minutes, while the mountain road used by the bus was sometimes blocked in winter. If BR needed an effective way of reducing patronage for its services, none better could be found. Cymmer nominally retained a rail link with Treherbert via this dreadful service until 14 December 1970, when it too was withdrawn. It is amazing that it survived for the best part of three years.

D. Pontrhydyfen to Efail-fâch
The last line to enter the Afan Valley was built by the Port Talbot Railway & Dock Company, which was incorporated on 31 July 1894. The company's Act authorized improvements to the dock at Port Talbot together with a railway line into the nearby Garw Valley, where colliery owners wanted access to a better port than the tidal harbour at Porthcawl. The new line ran from Port Talbot to Pontyrhyl (south of Blaengarw) and was opened throughout on 14 February 1898. Further Acts in 1896 authorized extensions to Cefn Junction on the GWR's Porthcawl branch, Aberavon and Tonmawr Junction on the SWMR. 'Our' line is the last of these. It opened to freight traffic on 14 November 1898, but the date of passenger opening is unknown.

While the general thrust of the PTR was eastwards, the branch to Tonmawr Junction was an exception: it started at Tonygroes North Junction, just outside Port Talbot, and headed north-east up the Afan Valley. As the Rhondda & Swansea Bay Railway had already claimed much of the west side of the valley, the PTR ran up the east side as far as Pontrhydyfen where it swung north into the Pelena Valley via the attractive brick-built Pontrhydyfen Viaduct. A mile and a half beyond, it met the South Wales Mineral Railway which it paralleled to Tonmawr Junction, where the two systems met. As noted earlier, this connection was a life saver for the SWMR, for it provided a route to a modern port which avoided the incline at Ynys-y-Maerdy.

The underlying philosophy of the PTR was to steal trade from the harbour at Porthcawl by offering better facilities at Port Talbot – hence its expansion eastwards. The success of this can be judged by that fact that it ended up serving over fifty separate collieries. On the other hand, such a policy risked antagonizing the mighty GWR, which had hitherto enjoyed an unchallenged monopoly in the area between Port Talbot and Bridgend. One might have expected the GWR to go on the offensive but instead it went out of its way to assist the new company, perhaps realizing that access to an improved harbour at Port Talbot was a lot cheaper than a prolonged fight over the inferior facilities at Porthcawl. In any event, this generous response established the friendly relations which culminated in the GWR working both the PTR and SWMR from 1908 onwards. In both cases, the GWR guaranteed generous dividends while leaving the local companies nominally independent. It formally absorbed them in 1922 and 1923 respectively.

Goods services over the Afan Valley line were withdrawn in February 1927. Passenger services followed on 22 September 1930, after which the line carried nothing but coal. On 9 May 1954, a new connection was made with the R&SBR south of Pontrhydyfen, which enabled the duplicate PTR route in the lower part of the valley to be abandoned. The rest of the line closed on 2 November 1964.

The Lines Today

After closure, most of the lines in the Afan Valley were acquired by West Glamorgan County Council and the Forestry Commission. The spur for their redevelopment as cycle trails was the publication in January 1982 of the so-called Grimshaw Report, a thirty-three volume *magnum opus* entitled *A Study of Disused Railways in England and Wales*. This identified a number of desirable and easily achievable routes in both countries including a

72 mile trail from Newport to Swansea, much of which was already in public ownership.

By June 1982, the West Glamorgan County Planning Committee had given its support to the Newport–Swansea route (and to a proposed cycle hire facility in the Afan Valley) and construction work started shortly afterwards using up to four teams employed under the former Manpower Services Commission Community Programme. The MSC paid for most of the labour, while grant aid for materials was supplied by the Countryside Commission and the Welsh Development Agency, especially where derelict land was involved. The biggest single work was the replacement of a demolished river bridge east of Pontrhydyfen at a cost of £24,000.

The first 10 miles of the present network were opened in the summer of 1985, together with the new cycle hire facility. Despite the unprecedented wetness of that summer, the venture was a great success with over 2,000 hirings being made. At a special opening event on 17 July that year, Waggy Woodpecker (a luckless soul dressed up in a cumbersome, outsize bird outfit) led a group of pupils from nearby Duffryn Primary School down the line on their bicycles. Since then, the network has been extended to include Abergwynfi and Glyncorrwg, while further extensions are planned to Cwmafan, Briton Ferry and Port Talbot. These have been on the drawing board for some time now – like the extensions west to Swansea and east to Newport – but work is progressing slowly. Like all such projects, they are hampered at a time of recession by lack of money and staff time.

The Walk (14 Miles)

As noted above, the disused lines in the Afan Valley provide a network of walking and cycling routes rather than a single, linear path. While the linear distance of the paths is 14 miles, an itinerary covering every last piece of disused railway in the valley is nearer 20 miles. The two main trails run along opposite sides of the valley from Cymmer to Pontrhydyfen, with short branches to Efail-Fâch, Glyncorrwg and Blaengwynfi.

The best place to start an exploration of the lines is from the Afan Argoed Country Park Visitor Centre. This is situated just west of Cynonville on the A4107 Port Talbot–Cymmer road (GR 821950). The facilities include the Welsh Miners' Museum, the Colliers' Café and Afan Argoed Cycle Hire Centre, which operates out of a restored Southern Railway covered wagon parked on the trackbed. There are also public conveniences and a free car park. It is worth spending some time here as there are plenty of industrial relics, including the pit wheel from the last colliery in Maesteg (closed in

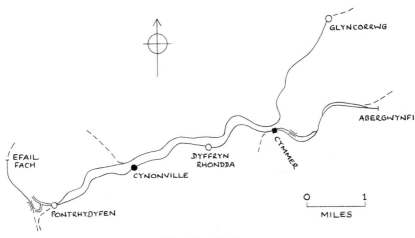

The Afan Valley

1985) and the inscription stone from the Rhondda Tunnel which reads: 'R. & S.B. RY. RHONDDA TUNNEL. LENGTH 3443 YARDS. OPENED JULY 1890.'

There are two routes from the visitor centre to the trackbed, but the trail along the south side of the A4107 is the safer as the road passes above it via a substantial girder bridge. Once on the trackbed, turn right for Afan Argoed Cycle Hire Centre and Cynonville Halt. The halt still retains its single platform, although the original buildings have been replaced by a modern, stone-built 'Barbecue Shelter'; the word 'shelter' implies that weather in the valley can be wet, which it certainly was when I visited. The platform has also been decorated with boundary markers from local railway companies such as the Great Western and the Rhondda & Swansea Bay company.

After this short diversion, I turned round and proceeded west down the valley. It is just over 1½ miles to Rhyslyn (GR 802943), where the line crosses the Afon Afan via a hybrid bridge, consisting of a modern span supported by the original stone abutments. This leads to a car park and picnic area (formerly the site of Pontrhydyfen station) where the trail leaves the trackbed in favour of the old station road, which can be followed into the village. If you wish to explore the short section from Pontrhydyfen to Efail-fâch, follow this road as far as GR 796943 and there turn left on to Bont Fawr Aqueduct, which has been tarmacked over. At the end of the aqueduct, proceed straight ahead via a residential road. Follow this as it turns sharp right (GR 796940) and then proceed to the end of the road (793940), keeping the local school on your right. The road now turns sharp left by a rough grassed area, where a tarmacked path will be seen on the

An imposing view of the brick-built Pontrhydyfen Viaduct, which carried the Port Talbot Railway out of the Afan and into the Pelenna Valley. This route was a veritable lifeline for the nearby South Wales Mineral Railway, which used it after opening in 1898 to avoid the costly Ynys-y-Maerdy Incline east of Briton Ferry

Author

right. This leads to the trackbed, which is gained by the south end of Pontrhydyfen Viaduct.

In railway terms, this viaduct is a modern structure, for it is brick- rather than stone-built. It consists of ten 40 ft spans and rises to a height of 70 ft above the valley. Having followed the Rhondda & Swansea Bay line from Cynonville, we are now on the trackbed of the Port Talbot Railway, travelling north towards Tonmawr Junction and the South Wales Mineral Railway. The modern path can be followed for 1¼ miles to the tiny village of Efail-fâch, where it stops just before a demolished bridge over the B4281 (GR 787954). Efail-fâch may be small, but it still has a bus service to Neath and a pub which is situated conveniently near the end of the trail. Having climbed a stiff gradient all the way from Pontrhydyfen, it is a relief to turn round and go the other way; cyclists will hardly need to turn their pedals.

It is now a case of retracing your steps as far as the car park at Rhyslyn (GR 801943). This time, however, instead of crossing the hybrid bridge and returning via the R&SBR, keep to the north side of the valley. The first section, from Rhyslyn to the east side of Gyfylchi Tunnel, is perhaps the most unusual stretch of abandoned railway in the whole valley. The line here was authorized by the R&SBR Act of 1892, the aim being to divert coal traffic from Glyncorrwg to Port Talbot or Swansea via R&SBR metals. The link was completed in 1899 but was never officially opened due to the close relationship which developed between the SWMR and the new PTR, which had reached Tonmawr Junction at the other end of Gyfylchi Tunnel a year earlier. The new line accordingly remained unused throughout its life. The R&SBR was authorized to dismantle the junction near the tunnel in 1915, but retained part of the line at the south end for use as a long siding from Pontrhydyfen station. It is still shown as such on the 1948 Ordnance Survey map.

As far as is possible to judge from old maps and the limited evidence on the ground, the junction between the R&SBR and SWMR was situated at GR 821954, roughly opposite Cynonville Halt on the east side of the valley. A path leads west from this point to the tunnel portal, which has been bricked up in the interests of safety. If you are determined, it is possible to get in but a visit is not recommended given that part of the tunnel roof collapsed in 1947! It is now plain sailing all the way to Cymmer; Brunel's clever contour-following means that the gradients for the next three miles are negligible. A rock cutting at grid reference 845959 is particularly noteworthy. On the approach to Cymmer, the view up the valley is dominated by the iron viaduct which once linked the SWMR with the GWR's Llynfi Valley branch; this remained in use until the final closure of Glyncorrwg Colliery in 1970.

At Cymmer, the SWMR crosses the lane to Abercregan at GR 859963; Cymmer Corrwg station lies immediately beyond on the left, set into a high

Cynonville Halt on the former Rhondda & Swansea Bay line from Treherbert to Swansea, with a group of Railway Ramblers in attendance. The two platforms are original, but the shelter on the right-hand side is a modern addition built to facilitate barbecues in the rain – a telling admission about the Welsh weather!

John Gibberd

cliff face. This was a rather inhospitable station, whose simple building did not even possess a canopy to protect intending passengers from the rain. The only other facility was a gents toilet at the north end of the platform. Today, only the crumbling platform edge and the back of the stone building remain.

At this point, the SWMR turned sharply north to follow the valley of the Afon Corrwg. The trackbed appears to have been used as a haul road in recent years, but is extremely easy to follow. Along the way, there is much evidence of landscaping by the Welsh Development Agency, no doubt trying to make good the scars created by former industry in the valley. The remote village of Glyncorrwg lies two and a half miles north of Cymmer. Its simple station once stood on the west side of the track at grid reference 874993, but there is no trace of it today.

Glyncorrwg boasts a few shops, two pubs, a café and a bus service, but it has clearly seen better days. A number of shops and residential properties are boarded up, suggesting that the place is becoming depopulated following the closure of the local mines. The railway continued north-east for another 2 miles to North Rhondda Halt, where the unadorned timber platform did not even possess a nameboard. From this point, branches fanned out to various mine workings, all of which were closed many years ago. I stopped at the site of Glyncorrwg station, purchased some confectionery in the local café and walked back to Cymmer. The incessant rain discouraged a longer stay, but if you have time, it might be worth seeing if traces remain of the line to North Rhondda. It is hard to imagine that anyone else has found a use for it in this remote valley.

Back in Cymmer, turn left on reaching the lane to Abercregan, then right on to the modern road bridge which crosses the valley at GR 860963. The 'Refreshment Room' from Cymmer Afan station stands at the south end of this bridge, still serving the purpose for which it was built in March 1888 – a handy place for a drink and a lucky survivor given the demolition which has been inflicted on the rest of the station area. Two railways proceeded east of this point: the Rhondda & Swansea Bay line to Treherbert, and the GWR line to Abergwynfi. Above Cymmer, the Afan Valley is very narrow and the two routes run side by side, following every twist and turn in the valley's sinuous course.

At GR 862961, the two lines pass under the minor road from Cymmer to Glyncorrwg. The separate bridges of the different companies are clearly visible, the R&SBR on the left and the GWR on the right. The R&SBR line is the most interesting to follow, for it runs on to Croeserw Viaduct which spans the Afon Gwynfi. It is tempting to think of damage to the parapets being caused by local vandals, but old photographs show that some of the coping stones have been missing for years – the result of an accident in 1946 when a miners' train ran off the rails and plunged into the valley. Fortunately, there were no serious injuries other than the driver's broken leg, but the noise of the accident (at 6.15 in the morning) woke up everyone in the village. Half a mile later, the line plunges into Gelli Tunnel, a real rarity on a line which follows a South Wales valley. The tunnel is still open and can be walked without difficulty, but a bridge at the east end has been demolished. Anyone choosing this route will be forced to retrace their steps to the west end of the tunnel, where a new path leads down on to the nearby GWR Abergwynfi branch.

The two lines then run side by side for another mile to the outskirts of Blaengwynfi (GR 885968), where they are blocked by road building and a new housing estate. This is literally the end of the line for the R&SBR, for its course to the southern portal of the Rhondda Tunnel has been obliterated. However, the GWR line can be traced for another ½ mile to the western edge of Abergwynfi. This is not one of the official Afan Argoed trails, but a clearly defined path shows that it is well used by locals.

Far from home. This Southern Railway parcels van, parked on a short stretch of track west of Cynonville Halt, now serves as the headquarters of Afan Argoed Cycle Hire. Cynonville is a good place on which to base a visit to the Afan Valley as there are many other facilities nearby, including the South Wales Miners' Museum, the Colliers' Café, a new Countryside Centre, several picnic sites and a touring caravan park

Author

Once again, the walker must retrace his steps, but this time the GWR trackbed can be followed. While this avoids Gelli Tunnel, it crosses a couple of minor bridges and affords a good view of the navvies' cottages built overlooking the line below Croeserw. On reaching Cymmer, stay on the main trail which passes the Refreshment Rooms and the south end of the iron viaduct. Here the GWR line turned south, plunging into the inky depths of Cymmer Tunnel, but nothing remains of its trackbed or the tunnel portal. The continuation of the cycle trail is along the course of the Rhondda & Swansea Bay line, which can now be followed back to Cynonville Halt and the Afan Argoed Visitor Centre.

It is 3 miles back to Cynonville and downhill all the way – a real treat on a bike. Nothing remains of Duffryn Rhondda Halt, although a set of substantial brick abutments in the vicinity are a tangible reminder of the past. (These were probably associated with Duffryn Rhondda Colliery, which closed in October 1966.) The line runs below Cynonville for ¼ mile before reaching its station, and then the walker has come full circle. Having passed the platform, barbecue shelter, boundary markers and the Afan

Argoed Cycle Hire Centre in its Southern Railway covered wagon, there is little more to do now other than make for the Colliers' Café and order a steaming pot of tea.

Further Explorations

Outside the main network of cycle trails in the Afan Valley, few trackbeds have been converted for recreational use, although I suspect the line from Glyncorrwg to North Rhondda can be walked with ease; in 1985, it was still owned by the local authority. To judge from old maps and photographs, not even sheep farmers could make a living in this bleak and lonely terrain. The presence of a large colliery at the head of the valley must have come as quite a shock for anyone unaware of its existence; it certainly made an incongruous sight, with the pit wheels set against the backdrop of a barren, scrub-covered mountain.

Two sections of old line survive in less dramatic surroundings. The first lies east of Briton Ferry, where the SWMR's Ynys-y-Maerdy Incline has been incorporated in a park; the old trackbed runs from GR 743949 to 766952 and enables walkers to judge firsthand the difficulties of working loaded coal trains down the slope. The other lies east of Port Talbot, where 3¼ miles of the old PTR line to Pontyrhyl survive as a railway path from Goytre (GR 781897) to Bryn (819920), thanks to the good offices of the Forestry Commission. Elsewhere walkers must use their initiative. West Glamorgan has an extremely rich industrial heritage and those willing to look will find plenty of interest. In an area where even some of the roads are built on old tramways, one does not necessarily have to look very far.

Transport and Facilities

Maps: Ordnance Survey: Landranger Series Sheet 170

Buses: Brewers Motor Services, The Travelshop,
           Bus Station, Port Talbot, West Glamorgan
           Telephone: Port Talbot (0639) 882181

           South Wales Transport, Quadrant Bus Station,
           1 Plymouth Street, Swansea, SA1 3QF
           Telephone: Swansea (0792) 475511

West Glamorgan County Council, Environment & Highways, County Hall, Swansea, SA1 3SN
Telephone: Swansea (0792) 471127 (direct line)

Trains: British Rail Telephone Enquiry Bureau
Telephone: Swansea (0792) 467777

Cycle Hire: Afan Argoed Cycle Hire, Afan Argoed Country Park, Cynonville, Port Talbot, West Glamorgan, SA13 3HG
Telephone: Cymmer (0639) 850564

Hire charges are £2.50 per hour for a mountain bike subject to a maximum of £10 (1994). There are reductions for children's bicycles. The hire centre is open throughout the year but at weekends only from November to March, when the number of bicycles is limited. Please telephone beforehand.

Once again, South Wales scores with good public transport. Brewers' service number 23 runs from Port Talbot to Blaengwynfi every hour. The main stops are Pontrhydyfen, Afan Argoed Country Park, Duffryn Rhondda and Cymmer. South Wales Transport operates a separate service from Swansea and Neath (number 235), which connects with the Afan Valley buses at Pontrhydyfen. Glyncorrwg is generally served by buses running to and from Maesteg in the Llynfi Valley, but these too connect with the Afan Valley buses at Cymmer. All of these services run until 11.00 p.m., Mondays to Saturdays, but there are no Sunday buses at all.

On the refreshments side, most of the villages in the Afan Valley have at least one pub each. The main 'watering holes' are at Blaengwynfi, Cymmer, Glyncorrwg, Duffryn Rhondda, Pontrhydyfen and Efail-fâch. Unfortunately, however, Welsh Brewers, the local Bass subsidiary, have a stranglehold on the area and there is little real choice.

Gelli Tunnel on the former Rhondda & Swansea Bay line from Briton Ferry to Treherbert was relatively short but built on a curve so that no light could be seen from the other end. The last train passed through in June 1960 but the tunnel is still there, and open, to satisfy the curiosity of inquisitive walkers

Kenfig Hill Community Route is built on part of the former GWR Porthcawl branch, which began life as a 4 ft 7 in tramway opened in 1829. An attractive feature of the route is that all the access points have been built in the style of level-crossings, which is particularly appropriate here as this *was* a level-crossing until 1973

David James Photography (Sussex)

8
THE OGMORE VALLEY
The Llynfi & Ogmore Railway

Introduction

The ancient market town of Bridgend is situated approximately midway between Cardiff and Swansea on the main line of the former South Wales Railway. Immediately to the north lies the bulk of the Glamorgan mountains, incised by the valleys Llynfi, Garw and Ogmore – once a very productive part of the Welsh coalfield. In the nineteenth century this area was dominated by the local Llynfi & Ogmore Railway, whose tentacles radiated out from Tondu where it established its headquarters, workshops and a substantial locomotive shed. In recent years, British Rail has revived part of this network by reintroducing a passenger service between Bridgend and Maesteg, but much of the rest has been bereft of passengers for many years and faces an uncertain future. (The dramatic decline of the local coal industry has not helped.) On the other hand, railway lines closed in the 1980s and 1990s have generally been treated more imaginatively than their counterparts in previous decades, and Ogwr Groundwork Trust, assisted by Ogwr Borough Council, is making commendable progress in establishing an integrated network of walks and cycleways based on disused L&OR lines. Just like the railway before it, this network will be based on Tondu – a case of history turning full circle, even if Shanks's pony has now replaced the iron horse.

History

The origins of the Llynfi & Ogmore Railway can be traced back to the Dyffryn Llynfi & Porthcawl Railway, an early dock and railway company which obtained its Act on 10 June 1825. This authorized a tramway of about 17 miles from Dyffryn Llynfi (north of Maesteg) to Porthcawl, where a pier and other harbour works were to be constructed. As this Act preceded that for the Llanelly Dock & Railroad Company by three years, Porthcawl can legitimately claim to be the first 'railway port'. The company's engineer was John Hodgkinson, who had earlier worked on the famous Hay Railway from Brecon to Eardisley.

The line was built to the rather odd gauge of 4ft 7in and opened in 1829; the permanent way consisting of iron rails spiked to stone block sleepers. The 'trains' are reputed to have been hauled by teams of three horses in the charge of a man and a lad, the latter being responsible for working the hand-points along the way. A rudimentary timetable was operated in order to ensure that trains did actually cross in the passing loops provided for this purpose, but it seems that confrontations still occurred on the single track. According to local tradition, the question of who had right of way was usually settled by a fight between the two lads.

The growth of the iron and coal industries around Cefn Cribwr and Maesteg ensured that the tramway was kept busy, but it had a limited capacity and soon proved unable to cope with the volume of traffic. It could accommodate only eight return trains per day, including those which covered just part of the route, and the average speed was a mere 3 m.p.h. It is hardly surprising, therefore, that local industrial interests grouped together to form the Llynfi Valley Railway, which was authorized on 7 August 1846 to acquire and improve the DL&PR which it duly purchased on 22 July 1847. Seven years later, the LVR also acquired the Bridgend Railway, which in 1834 had opened a connecting line from Park Slip (near Cefn Cribwr) to Bridgend. However, not for the first time in Victorian railway history, ambition exceeded achievement. The LVR produced only a modest surplus, despite the high tolls charged on its lines, and was unable to rebuild them with heavier rails and metal chairs in order to allow locomotive working.

The company tackled this problem in 1855 by obtaining a further Act which authorized the rebuilding of its tramways as broad gauge railways. Unfortunately, it took another three years to raise the necessary finance, partly because the money market was tight during and immediately after the Crimean War. However, the company published a successful prospectus in February 1858 and this, coupled with a 6 per cent dividend to encourage wavering shareholders, finally did the trick. The final, tragic problem was the appointment of I.K. Brunel as engineer, for he died on the job in 1859, his health ruined as a result of anxiety caused by the monumental Great Eastern project.

Despite all the difficulties, the LVR finally opened a broad gauge railway from Dyffryn Llynfi to Porthcawl on 10 August 1861, on which date steam locomotives finally replaced horses as the motive power. (As a matter of interest, this was largely a new line, as much of the tramway route – especially north of Tondu – was much too tortuous for a proper railway.) However, the opening brought little comfort to James Brogden, a partner in the Tondu Ironworks, who was angered that the LVR failed to install a connection to his factory. His initial reaction was to claim compensation, but, disappointed with the sum he received in settlement, he set about promoting the Ogmore Valley Railway instead. The Act for this was passed on 13 July 1863 and authorized a standard gauge line from Nantymoel to Tondu, with running powers over the LVR line to Porthcawl via a specially laid third rail. These works were rapidly completed, with passenger and freight services from Nantymoel to Porthcawl commencing on 1 August 1865. Three locomotives were purchased for the opening, together with no less than five hundred wagons from the Lancaster Wagon Co., which makes it clear where the new railway expected its profits to come from – coal.

Different historians see different trends in the companies' affairs at this time. Some point to the OVR's acquisition of the Ely Valley Extension Railway, with its connections to Llantrisant and Cardiff, and suggest that this posed a threat to the LVR's maritime trade at Porthcawl; others maintain that they were already co-operating closely, as witnessed by their joint enlargement of Porthcawl harbour under an Act of 1864. On balance, the case for co-operation is strongest, not least because by 1865 the Brogden family was represented on both boards of directors: Alexander on the LVR, and Alexander, Henry, James and John on the OVR. In any event, the two companies amalgamated by an Act dated 28 June 1866 to form the Llynfi & Ogmore Railway.

The first issue to be tackled by the new company was the one of gauge and, by 1868, all its broad gauge lines had been fitted with a third rail. It re-equipped itself with standard gauge locomotives and rolling stock, but retained the broad gauge where it existed in order to facilitate traffic exchange with the Great Western, which was dragging its feet over the issue. (As in parts of Devon, this gave rise to the odd sight of a standard gauge locomotive hauling trains of mixed gauge.) Profits were good, particularly on the OVR line from Nantymoel, and the GWR began to take an interest. This culminated in the L&OR receiving an offer that was too good to refuse: in return for working and managing the line, the GWR would pay all dividends on the preference shares plus a guaranteed 6 per cent minimum dividend on the ordinary shares. Additionally, it would continue building extensions to the network which had already been started. The directors accepted, and full absorption followed ten years later on 1 July 1883.

The subsequent history of these lines is somewhat less eventful, and writers have tended to concentrate on the Porthcawl branch due to the town's extraordinary transformation from industrial harbour to seaside resort. In essence, the docks at Porthcawl were not very good: they were

A classic picture of a South Wales branch line terminus: Nantymoel, at the head of the Ogmore Valley. The small timber building is a reminder that in most of the valleys, passengers were served as an afterthought – coal was the real king. Even so, little stations such as this would have been busy enough on Saturday nights when the last train from Bridgend returned with its human cargo – miners who had been to town for their beer

Mike Hitches

tidal, relatively shallow and offered little room for expansion. These disadvantages were immaterial in the early nineteenth century but became acute as ships grew larger; and as soon as better facilities were opened at Barry and Port Talbot, Porthcawl's business disappeared. The GWR closed the harbour in 1898, although some residual trade appears to have lingered on until 1906. After that, the railway filled in the inner basin and built upon it a new passenger station, which opened on 6 March 1916.

Officially, the Porthcawl branch started at Tondu but the most intensive service was provided between Porthcawl and Pyle, where local trains usually made main line connections. In 1910, the number of journeys from Pyle to Tondu was only four, although this had increased to six by 1922. In 1953, the intensive service between Porthcawl and Pyle was extended to Kenfig Hill, worked by a push-and-pull unit as that station had no run-round facilities. By all accounts a trip over the branch was a noisy affair: the line was still tortuous, reflecting its tramway origins, and the wheels of both locomotives and rolling stock screeched around many of the curves. This produced such exaggerated wear on the flanges of the locomotives' wheels that the staff at Tondu shed (86F) had to turn the engines round at midday to even it out.

By the early 1960s, the small amount of passenger traffic on the Tondu–Kenfig Hill section made it a deserving candidate for closure, but the fact that British Railways proposed to close with it the whole line to Porthcawl was controversial to say the least. Apart from a large number of summer excursions, the town enjoyed a good commuter business with daily trains running to and from Swansea and Cardiff, and just a few years earlier BR had announced plans to construct a brand new station – hardly the picture of a line in decline. However, railways were in a bad position at the time, pushed back by a flood of motor vehicles and motorway building. The Tondu–Porthcawl passenger service was accordingly withdrawn on 9 September 1963, with Pyle–Porthcawl freight services following on 1 February 1965. Freight services from Cefn Junction (west of Tondu) to Pyle survived until 19 November 1973.

The line from Tondu to Nantymoel fared rather better, although railway historians have tended to neglect it. Passenger services after the turn of the century were fairly light, although they were an improvement on those between Tondu and Pyle. Five or six trains generally ran up the valley, with one more coming down. Conditional trains were also a feature of the line, with extra services running variously on Wednesdays, Fridays and Saturdays. On top of this, there were several colliers' specials and the branch's mainstay – coal trains. Local coal production received a tremendous boost following the outbreak of World War II, reaching a peak of 3 million tons per annum in the mid-1950s. After this, the decline was slower than in other parts of the coalfield because British Railways continued to use large quantities of locally mined steam coal.

Passenger services between Tondu and Nantymoel were withdrawn on 5 May 1958, with goods services beating a steady retreat down the valley between 1962 and 1965. After that, the line remained open to serve the combined Wyndham/Western Colliery at Nantymoel and the large washeries at Ogmore Vale. Final closure accompanied the decline of the coal industry; the section from Nantymoel to Caedu Crossing closed on 21 October 1983, with the remainder from Caedu to Tondu following on 16 July 1986. It is hard to imagine now, but as recently as 1971, Wyndham/Western Colliery employed 1,188 men and produced the coalfield record of 474,874 tons of saleable coal. Soon, the 'greening of the valleys' will have removed all trace of this. Although this is no bad thing in itself, it is hard to imagine how the local economy can cope with job losses on so large a scale.

The Lines Today

The abandoned line from Cefn Junction to Pyle had to wait no less than nineteen years before anything constructive was done with it, but in spring

1992 work finally began on creating the modern 'community route'. Further work continued intermittently from 1992–4, with the trail finally opening throughout in April 1994. The project was co-ordinated by Ogwr Borough Council, which obtained 80 per cent grant aid from the Welsh Development Agency – a factor which enabled construction to be completed very rapidly at a time of local authority cutbacks. Part of the work was carried out by a group of International Volunteers, who came from countries as diverse as Ghana, Russia and Spain.

The disused line from Nantymoel to Tondu was fortunate in that it escaped similar neglect. The rails from Nantymoel to Ogmore Vale had been lifted by 1990, although those from Ogmore Vale to Tondu remained in place until about 1992. However, lifting then began in earnest and, by August 1993, all that remained was a mile and a half of rusty, overgrown track from Tondu to just east of Brynmenyn. Ogwr Groundwork Trust built the modern cycle trail very promptly. The first phase from Nantymoel to Ogmore Vale was completed in July 1992 and the second, from Ogmore Vale to just short of Brynmenyn opened exactly a year later. Further extensions are planned in due course.

Within a period of just over two years, nearly 9 miles of derelict railway land have been turned into two popular and well-used walks-cum-cycleways. Much of the credit for this lies with Ogwr Borough Council, which commissioned a report in 1990 to 'examine the immediate needs and potential for path development, together with specific recommendations for action'. As a result, it had a very clear idea of the opportunities that existed, and what needed to be done to realize them. Let us hope that many other local authorities will follow this example.

Walk 1 – Nantymoel to Brynmenyn (6½ miles)

Nantymoel is about as far up the Ogmore Valley as you can get. A mile or so beyond, the valley comes to an abrupt end and there's nothing left but a steep climb up Craig Ogwr. The village was created in the 1870s to serve the Ocean Western Colliery, which was sunk in 1872 by David Davies & Co. The colliery was situated to the east of the village at GR 938927, but there is no point in looking for it today as it has been landscaped out of existence. However, the abutments of a demolished bridge at GR 936924 reveal the course of the branch line which once served it.

The modern railway path starts at the site of Nantymoel station, which stood at GR 933930. Nothing remains of the platform or buildings but the site is overlooked by the backs of neighbouring properties, as was *de rigeur*

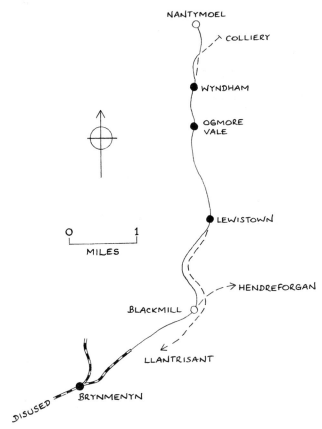

NANTYMOEL

COLLIERY

WYNDHAM

OGMORE VALE

LEWISTOWN

HENDREFORGAN

BLACKMILL

LLANTRISANT

BRYNMENYN

DISUSED

O _____ 1

MILES

The Ogmore Valley

for railway stations everywhere. A modern barrier, designed to keep out horse riders and motorcyclists, gives access to the trail. The line runs downhill on a steep falling gradient, passing a children's play area on the left and crossing a low bridge over the River Ogwr at GR 935926. Shortly after this, it meets the junction for Ocean Western Colliery at GR 934923 before running past Wyndham Colliery immediately beyond. (These two collieries were amalgamated in 1965 to form Wyndham/Western Colliery, referred to in the History section.) However, neither the junction nor Wyndham Colliery can be seen as the area has been landscaped and the trail diverted to the right; it regains the trackbed at the north end of Wyndham village. Features of note here are the level-crossing at GR 933918 (complete with a point preserved in the road) and the solitary platform of Wyndham Halt at GR 933916.

Ogmore Vale on the Llynfi & Ogmore Railway was an important station on the line from Tondu to Nantymoel. Always busy with local coal traffic, it was also important in railway terms as the end of the double track section from Caedu Crossing. Today, the station site has been turned into a small local park, presided over by this towering signal
David James Photography (Sussex)

The station at Ogmore Vale is reached in another ½ mile at GR 933907. This was a place of some importance, as revealed by the large station site. Two platforms survive, together with several posts from the level crossing and a well preserved signal. This is so well preserved, in fact, that it might be a modern interloper. Just north of the station, another colliery branch ran in from the east. Traffic from this and other collieries on the line no doubt justified the provision of double track for the next mile and a half to Caedu Crossing (GR 935882). South of the station, the line has a very urban look as it negotiates a long curve to the left, passing the backs of nearby houses. It finally reaches open country again at the site of another level-crossing at GR 934896.

There is now an attractive view to the south with the trees of Ogmore Forest spilling down the east side of the valley; but what caught my attention was a vast, blackened area to the left of the line which used to accommodate the local coal washeries. No doubt this area was already scheduled for landscaping, but its sheer size (150 yd wide by half a mile long) made it clear that the collieries in the valley had a vast output. At the south end, I was surprised to discover a row of concrete lamp posts which must have illuminated the sidings at night.

After a barrier south of the washeries, the line becomes very rural and enclosed. At GR 935882, it crosses the Ogmore River on a low bridge before reaching the diminutive platform of Lewistown Halt at GR 932878. South of the halt, the line crosses the river again before passing the site of Cardiff & Ogmore Junction, where a little known freight line branched off on the left for Bryncethin Junction, Llantrisant and Cardiff. This had a very short life as a through route, opening in 1876 and closing in 1938. After the junction, the main trail passes under a large concrete road bridge (built to last but with few aesthetic considerations) before crossing the river for the last time and reaching the site of Blackmill station (GR 933864). If you fancy a stop for refreshments, the tiny village of Blackmill is recommended as it has more than its fair share of pubs: turn left a quarter of a mile before the station at the site of an old level-crossing (GR 933867). Suspecting a railway connection, I made for the Ogmore Junction, a friendly, busy local with a garden and patio. From the latter, the abutment of a demolished viaduct can be seen, nestling in the trees on the far side of the A4061 – part of the short-lived Cardiff & Ogmore line to Bryncethin Junction.

As the pub name suggests, Blackmill was once a railway junction but it lost this status in 1961 when a 3½ mile link to Hendreforgan (shorn of its passenger service in 1930) was closed also to freight. This short line provided another route from the Ogmore Valley to Llantrisant and Cardiff, although passenger trains only ever operated between Blackmill and Hendreforgan, reversing there for a one mile climb to the mining village of Gilfach Goch. In 1922, this service consisted of five trains per day with a late night special on Wednesdays, Fridays and Saturdays, operated in conjunction with the 11.00 p.m. Bridgend–Nantymoel working which ran on the same nights. One can safely assume that these were the days when Gilfach and Nantymoel miners went to Bridgend for their beer.

Many visitors pass the site of Blackmill station without noticing it at all. The most obvious sign is the base of the signal-box, which stands about 18 in high on a grassy mound that used to be the platform. About 20 yd to the south, the twin posts that held the station nameboard are still in place. If you have time to root around in the vegetation, you can also trace the edge of the Gilfach branch platform and the remains of the bridge which carried that line over the nearby Ogmore River.

The trail beyond the station is idyllic, passing a mixture of broadleaved woodland and pasture with the river close at hand. In summer, a sweet scent fills the air and a quick glance to the left reveals countless Indian balsams lining the river bank and filling the nearby fields. These plants are very distinctive: they grow to a height of 5 ft or more and produce large pink flowers like those of the domestic antirrhinum.

On the occasion of my visit, the official path ended near a ford at GR 917855 but an extension to Brynmenyn is planned some time after this book is published. I pressed on down the old line for another mile, wading through swathes of Indian balsams on the way. Somehow, a few evening

This bridge south of Kenfig Hill on the disused Porthcawl branch clearly reveals the line's tramway origins. It is now a prominent feature on the Kenfig Hill Community Route, which has restored the empty trackbed to public use

Author

primroses had managed to gain a foothold in the ballast as well, and their bright yellow petals provided a welcome change of colour. The bridge carrying the A4065 over the line (GR 910849) was an extraordinary sight, being completely blocked with balsams which, by this time, I was beginning to regard as something of a mixed blessing.

Brynmenyn station stood nearby at GR 905848, just west of the junction with the Garw Valley line. If all goes according to plan, this too will become a cycle trail in the near future, as will the next mile of track leading to Tondu. However, walkers should not attempt this section until the cycle trail is established, as it leads on to the operational Bridgend–Maesteg line.

Walk 2 – Kenfig Hill Community Route (2¼ miles)

Note: It is proposed to link walks 1 and 2 as part of the local cycle trail network. Until this work is complete, a convenient footpath can be used which links Tondu and Aberkenfig with the western end of Cefn Cribwr. It runs from GR 893839 to 854837 and follows the north side of the Tondu–Port Talbot railway line.

The Kenfig Hill Community Route starts near the western end of Cefn Cribwr at GR 854834, where there is a small car park. If you are travelling north from the B4281, follow the signs to Bedford Park and keep an eye out for the White Lion pub, which is about 200 yd south of the start of the trail. Shortly after the pub, there is a small garden centre on the right, which is housed in a former crossing-keeper's cottage; the entrance to the car park follows immediately on the left.

Bedford Park is named after John Bedford, who established the ironworks situated just off the trail at GR 851834. They were developed in the 1770s and 1780s but Bedford died in 1791, after which the site gradually fell into disuse. The last attempt to make a success of ironmaking here failed in about 1836, although a brickworks and a colliery elsewhere on the estate remained in use until shortly after World War I. Anyone viewing the site today could be forgiven for thinking that they had stumbled upon the ruins of a medieval monastery. The buildings, including a furnace, an engine-house, a casting-house and a row of calcining kilns, were certainly constructed on a large scale. (The engine house supplied a constant flow of air to keep the furnace burning at a high temperature.) In 1987, they were acquired by Ogwr Borough Council, which carried out emergency repairs and recently started an archaeological excavation.

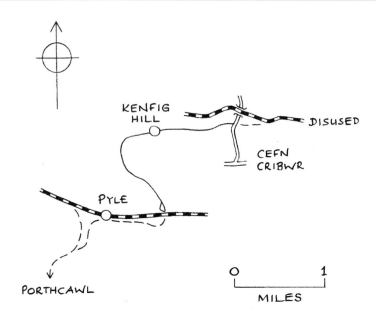

Kenfig Hill Community Route

Beyond the ironworks, the trail continues through broad-leaved woodland to the eastern edge of Kenfig Hill. The varieties here include oak, ash, hawthorn and hazel; indeed, the oak is so abundant that it has been used to make the sturdy picnic tables outside the ironworks. The trail reaches Kenfig Hill at the site of a level-crossing (GR 840833) which preceded the village station. The nearby Masons Arms, which must have had a few rail-borne patrons in its time, is a handy place for refreshments. It is a bit run down, but I found a big welcome and plenty of humour. Any visitor entering the bar with a camera is likely to be asked, 'Here, are you from the Social? Just look at this bloke, fit as a fiddle and he's been on the sick for six weeks.'

Beyond the Masons Arms, the trail switches to Station Road before regaining the old trackbed at GR 837833. The next section provides an excellent view to the north, while a tight curve to the south clearly reveals the line's tramway origins. There was a level-crossing at GR 833829, after which the line entered a cutting before burrowing under Bridge Street (the B4281 on the modern OS map). This cutting has long been filled in and is now presided over by the local health centre, the distinctive architecture revealing what the building is long before you can read the sign.

Beyond the health centre, the line plunges down a steep gradient as it

A picnic area near the east end of the Kenfig Hill Community Route overlooks these ruins, which one could easily mistake for an abandoned medieval monastery were it not for the unusual 'portholes' in the far wall. In fact, these are the remains of an ironworks developed by John Bedford in the eighteenth century. They have been derelict since about 1836, but are currently the subject of an archaeological study by Ogwr Borough Council

David James Photography (Sussex)

makes the final approach to Pyle. There is an ancient bridge at GR 840821, after which a branch of the trail forks off on the right. It doesn't matter which way you go here (both routes loop back to the bridge), but I continued straight ahead, staying on the old railway. The trackbed is used for about another ¼ mile, after which the path swings right to avoid a flooded section leading to a bridge under the Bridgend–Port Talbot main line (GR 841818). It then meanders through Frog Pond Local Nature Reserve before rejoining the trackbed by the railway bridge at GR 840821. You have now negotiated a reverse loop and are facing Kenfig Hill which lies three-quarters of a mile ahead, back the way you came.

Further Explorations

Unfortunately, this area contains no other railway walks apart from a few short sections of the line from Hendreforgan to Gilfach Goch, which have been absorbed into the local footpath network. Various abandoned lines are still largely extant (especially that from Blackmill to Gellirhiadd Junction), but they are probably in private ownership and are definitely not open to the public. Additionally, a few traces of the early Bridgend Railway are reputed to survive near the little village of Pen-y-fai (GR 89/82), notably a stone bridge which still bears its nineteenth-century builder's plaque.

In the long term, all this should change. Ogwr Borough Council intends to extend the two routes described above to Tondu, which will become the focus for many of the cycle trails now under development. Several of these will utilize sections of old railway, including the Garw Valley line from Brynmenyn to Blaengarw. The Kenfig Hill Community Route will also be extended to Kenfig Nature Reserve on the coast. As a matter of interest, the local plan identifies Bridgend as another focus of future cycle routes, with trails radiating out to Pencoed, Brynmenyn, Porthcawl and Ogmore by Sea. Obviously, not all of these will or even could be based on old railways, but if implemented, they will create one of the most extensive networks of off-road walking and cycling routes in South Wales.

Transport and Facilities

Maps: Ordnance Survey: Landranger Series Sheet 170

Buses: Brewers Motor Services, The Travelshop,
            Market Street, Bridgend, Mid Glamorgan
            Telephone: Bridgend (0656) 647093

            Porthcawl Omnibus Ltd.,
            Station Lane, Porthcawl, Mid Glamorgan
            Telephone: Porthcawl (0656) 783269

            Mid Glamorgan County Council, Public Transport Group,
            Highways & Transportation Department,
            Greyfriars Road, Cardiff, CF1 3LG
            Telephone: Cardiff (0222) 820626 (direct line)

Trains: British Rail Telephone Enquiry Bureaux
            Telephone: Cardiff (0222) 228000
                    or: Swansea (0792) 467777

Most buses in this area are operated by Brewers Motor Services and travel to and from Bridgend. (As a matter of interest, the bus station in Market

Street, Bridgend, is very close to the original terminus of the Bridgend Railway; the site is proposed for redevelopment and may shortly cease to exist, but a plaque on the nearby Kwiksave supermarket gives brief details of the tramway's history.) Routes serving the walks in this chapter are as follows:

12/14/15 Bridgend–Brynmenym–Blaengarw
20/21/22 Bridgend–Blackmill–Nantymoel
62/63 Bridgend–Cefn Cribwr–Kenfig Hill–Porthcawl

All of these services are excellent with a weekday frequency of never less than two buses per hour. There are predictable reductions in the evenings and on Sundays, but all routes operate until about 11 p.m., seven days a week.

Given that parts of these lines traverse fairly remote countryside – especially if you link them together by walking from Brynmenyn to Cefn Cribwr – facilities are rarely far away. Pubs are easily found at Nantymoel, Ogmore Vale, Blackmill, Brynmenyn, Tondu and Kenfig Hill, and there are even two between Aberkenfig and Cefn Cribwr – the Fountain at GR 883834 and the White Lion at GR 854834. Bass dominates the local scene but there are a few Brains' pubs and, commendably, some of the big brewers' houses offer Brains or Crown Buckley beers as 'guests'. Additionally, there are shops in Ogmore Vale, Tondu, Aberkenfig and Kenfig Hill. The cycle shop outside Ogmore Vale station is particularly useful now that the old railway is used as a cycle trail. I would not wish a puncture on any cyclist, but if you are unlucky enough to get one, let's hope it happens here!

9
THE TAFF TRAIL
Brecon to Cardiff

Introduction

The Taff Trail is currently the longest designated cycle route in the UK. Although the Trans Pennine Trail from Hull to Liverpool will eventually eclipse it in terms of distance, it offers a unique cross-section of the landscape and history of South Wales. It starts in Brecon, an attractive market town which still bears the imprint of its medieval history, and for the first 7 miles to Talybont-on-Usk runs alongside or close to the picturesque Monmouthshire & Brecon Canal. At Talybont it turns south, following first the Brynoer Tramway and then the Brecon & Merthyr Railway on a 7 mile climb over the mountains that separate the Usk Valley from Merthyr Tydfil.

Having reached Merthyr, the trail follows the Taff Vale all the way to Cardiff, utilizing sections of the Glamorganshire Canal, the Pennydarren Tramway and a short local line with probably the longest name in the history of South Wales transport – the Alexandra (Newport & South Wales) Docks & Railway Co. Further disused railways follow: the Rhymney Railway, the Barry Railway and the little known Melingriffith Tramway, before the trail rejoins the Glamorganshire Canal for its final run to Cardiff Castle.

It will be obvious that this route reuses a tremendous mileage of canals, tramways and railways, most of which had been long abandoned before the Taff Trail gave them a new purpose in life. The views along the way are varied and impressive to say the least: the lush meadows of the Usk Valley, the bare mountain tops above Merthyr Tydfil and the industrial heritage of the Taff Vale, arguably the most important of all the iron and coal producing valleys in South Wales. There is enough cycling here for up to three days, and enough walking for up to five: indeed, the more time you spend exploring the trail and its surroundings, the more you will get out of it.

History

A. The Brynoer Tramway

Like many early tramways in South Wales, the Brynoer Tramway was initially constructed as a feeder for a canal – the Brecknock & Abergavenny, which received its Act in March 1793. The B&A was promoted initially to build an independent line from Brecon to Newbridge, near Caerleon, but this would have duplicated the route of the earlier Monmouthshire Canal south of Pontypool. In the event, sensible counsels prevailed and the two companies agreed to create a single joint line with an end-on junction at Pontymoile. The B&A's Act also authorized the construction of connecting tramways up to 8 miles from the canal, but the company was fairly selective about the routes it built and frustrated a number of local business interests by denying them a connection.

Thus it was that a group of B&A shareholders in alliance with Benjamin Hall, a colliery owner at Brynoer near Rhymney, built the Brynoer Tramway themselves. The line started from wharves at Talybont and, after an arduous climb up the west flank of Tor y Foel, skirted around Cefn Crug before reaching Trefil Limestone Quarries. It then ran downhill to Brynoer Patch, north-east of Rhymney, where it made a connection with Hall's colliery. The total length of the line was about 12 miles and it opened in May or June 1815.

Southbound traffic consisted mainly of pit props, with coal and limestone going the other way. Unfortunately, the route taken by these minerals was unbelievably circuitous: most were bound for Newport, yet the first 12 miles of their journey (to Talybont, where they were transferred to canal barge) were in the opposite direction. This made the tramway particularly vulnerable to alternatives such as the 'old' Rumney Railway, which opened a direct line from Rhymney to Newport in 1836. A small amount of trade (presumably northbound to Brecon) survived this blow, but it seemed that a full revival might come when in 1861 a scheme for a Sirhowy & Brecknockshire Railway proposed to rebuild the line as a short cut to the Sirhowy Valley at Tredegar. However, it was not to be, and the tramway was next used to carry materials for the construction of the Brecon & Merthyr Railway. The B&M opened its line from Brecon to Dowlais in 1863, and this effectively sealed the tramway's fate; by 1865, it was dead on its feet.

B. The Brecon & Merthyr Railway

The Brecon & Merthyr Tydfil Junction Railway, to use its official title, was a pugnacious local concern that thought nothing of taking on the biggest and mightiest rivals in the land. The Victorian directors of many railways must have discussed the plots and proposals of this diminutive company as it sought to extend its power and influence, and as a result, it had an impact on the railway history of South Wales out of all proportion to its size.

The B&M was incorporated on 1 August 1859 and aimed from the start to reach the Bristol Channel rather than simply linking the towns named in its title. (It achieved this by its purchase of the 'old' Rumney Railway, which is discussed in greater detail in Chapter 10.) It opened a line from Brecon to Dowlais on 23 April 1863 with a horse-bus service to and from Merthyr meeting trains at Pant. This was an extraordinary railway, even by Victorian standards, for between Talybont-on-Usk and Torpantau it climbed 925 ft up the side of Tor y Foel by what became known as the Seven Mile Bank. In promoting the line, the company's 1858 prospectus declared blithely that 'a good locomotive road can be obtained throughout', a statement that sits ill at ease with subsequent tales of operating expense and 'wild runs': two or even three locomotives were sometimes needed to get trains up the bank, or control their descent, while runaways were relatively common, as became painfully clear in the inquest that followed the worst of them in 1878. The Victorians clearly were capable of turning optimism into a dangerous vice.

The horse-bus service from Pant underlined the company's intention of constructing a branch to Merthyr, and it had already obtained an Act for this when the Brecon–Dowlais service was inaugurated. (Gradients dictated

Another classic scene from the valleys – ex-GWR Collett 0–6–0 pannier tank No. 6423 hauls a passenger train across Cefn Coed viaduct in November 1957. The train is probably a local working from Pontsticill to Merthyr Tydfil

D.K. Jones

that Pontsticill rather than Pant was to become the junction station.) Work progressed slowly from 1862 until 1866, when the company's bankers, Overend & Gurney, collapsed with debts of £11 million. This dragged the B&M into insolvency and it remained in the hands of the Official Receiver for the next two years. The whole débâcle brought construction of the Merthyr branch to an abrupt halt, with the massive Cefn Coed Viaduct standing half-finished in mid air. Thankfully, the company's engineer, Alexander Sutherland, pressed ahead in these difficult circumstances and managed to open the line to Cefn Coed on 1 August 1867, with completion to Merthyr following exactly a year later. Six years later, in 1874, the B&M agreed to make the Merthyr branch joint with the LNWR (which was then pressing into South Wales with offshoots from its Heads of the Valleys line) in return for the larger company reimbursing 50 per cent of the construction costs at £25,000 per mile.

By this time, the B&M network was complete, although its evolution as two separate railways – the B&M proper and the 'old' Rumney – was reflected in working timetables which referred to them as the 'northern' and 'southern' sections respectively. In essence, the coal-carrying southern section made all the money, while the mountainous northern section with its horrendous gradients either side of Torpantau consumed it. It is a reflection on the incredible wealth of the Welsh coal trade that there was anything left at all, but in its last three years of existence (1918–21), the B&M managed a dividend of 4 per cent: rather meagre in comparison with the 9 per cent regularly declared by the Barry Railway, but commendable in view of the B&M's operating difficulties.

It is not surprising that the northern section attracted the most notable incidents. Immediately after opening, the B&M attempted (inadvertently, one hopes) to freeze its staff in Torpantau signal-box by failing to provide a fireplace – this was no joke in winter at a height of nearly 1,450 ft on a bare mountain top. The staff had to raise a petition for this basic necessity, which was grudgingly installed in 1868. Torpantau was also the scene of some tremendous blizzards, the worst of which occurred in 1947. On this occasion, a southbound passenger train from Brecon entered Torpantau Tunnel only to find that the southern portal had been blocked by an avalanche of snow. The crew stopped the engine and reversed slowly to the other end, only to discover that the same thing had happened there. The train remained entombed for several days, complete with women and children on board, until it was eventually dug out by troops from Brecon Barracks. Earlier rescue attempts failed abysmally: a rescue engine from Merthyr ran off the rails completely, such was the depth of snow, while jet engines loaned by the RAF proved unable to blast the portals clear. The train remained trapped for several days more, and the snow did not finally clear from the mountains until the following June.

The other spectacular incident here was the 'wild run' of 2 December 1878, referred to briefly above, in which a thirty-seven wagon train hauled by no less than three engines crashed to its doom near Talybont-on-Usk. In breach of regulations, the crew did not stop to pin down the brakes of their wagons, thinking perhaps that the weight of the three engines would be sufficient to control the load. It was a fatal mistake, and one that most of them paid for with their lives. The train gradually accelerated out of control and, by the time it rattled over the canal bridge at Talybont, was reckoned to be travelling at about 60 m.p.h. It then tore into a reverse curve with a normal speed limit of 40 m.p.h. before plunging off an embankment and killing four of the six crewmen. On the descent, the engines – which had been put into reverse in a desperate attempt to stop them – literally shook themselves to pieces: parts of their motion were found up to 2 miles from the scene of the final crash. At the inquest that followed, the frequency of these 'wild runs' was finally revealed, plus the fact that B&M crews habitually worked extremely long hours. The result was a series of severe restrictions on working the bank, which remained little changed until the line finally closed in 1962. Unfortunately, it took a lot longer for railwaymen's working hours to be reduced. In January 1882, fireman Charles Makepeace recorded in his log book that he worked almost ninety-eight hours in a single week. Figures like this make one appreciate why nineteenth-century working people so needed the trade unions.

The B&M was absorbed into the Great Western Railway on 1 July 1922 and became part of the Western Region of British Railways with nationalization in 1948. Passenger services were withdrawn between Pontsticill and Merthyr on 13 November 1961, with the main line from Brecon to Dowlais suffering the same fate on 31 December 1962. Freight services survived until 4 May 1964 but were then withdrawn with the exception of a 4 mile stub between Merthyr and Vaynor Quarry (near Pontsarn). This remained in use until 3 October 1966. Happily, part of the main line was revived on 8 June 1980, when the narrow gauge Brecon Mountain Railway began operating between Pant and Pontsticill. This company has leased the line all the way to the southern portal of Torpantau Tunnel and thus has plenty of room to expand, should it wish to do so.

C. The Pennydarren Tramway
Like the Brynoer Tramway, this early railroad was inextricably linked with a waterway – the famous Glamorganshire Canal, which at one time was arguably the busiest and most prosperous canal in the British Isles. Looking at the route of the Pennydarren Tramway today, one might think that it was built purely to serve the waterway, but it was conceived originally as an alternative.

The problem lay in the way the Glamorganshire Canal was managed. The Crawshay family, substantial investors in the canal and masters of the largest ironworks in Merthyr, were considered to be running it largely for their own benefit. (There is certainly evidence that they encouraged boat owners to take *their* cargoes rather than those of other Merthyr ironmasters.) This developed into a full scale feud, which resulted in the complainants being ejected from the board of directors. However, these were not men of straw, for they represented the Dowlais, Pennydarren and Plymouth ironworks. They responded in 1798 by promoting an independent tramway which was to run all the way from Cardiff to Merthyr with a number of connecting branches. The outcry from the canal company was predictable, but neither toll concessions nor the enforced withdrawal of their Parliamentary bill could break the dissidents' resolve. Having failed to obtain Parliamentary authority for their proposals, they proceeded without.

The line as finally built ran from a junction with the Dowlais Tramroad east of Merthyr to the canal basin at Abercynon. To this extent, it may be seen as something of a compromise. It no longer threatened traffic along the whole length of the canal, and what traffic it did obtain would be fed into the canal at Abercynon anyway. The tramway was 9½ miles long, had a gauge of 4 ft 2 in and opened throughout in 1802. It remained busy until the 1850s but then declined as railways stole its trade and local ironworks

Morlais Junction viewed from the top of Morlais Tunnel on 30 November 1957. The line in the foreground was built by the LNWR and led east to join the heavily engineered 'Heads of the Valleys' route to Abergavenny. The other lines are, on the right, the Brecon & Merthyr's branch to Pontsticill and, in the distance, the two companies' joint line to Merthyr Tydfil. Ex-GWR pannier tank No. 6423 is approaching with a local passenger working from Merthyr to Pontsticill. This spot is easily missed, especially if you are cycling south, i.e. downhill.

D.K. Jones

closed. The *coup de grâce* came in 1880 when the Plymouth Works gave up making iron. Thereafter, the section from Merthyr to Mount Pleasant was converted into a railway and the rest abandoned.

Despite its relatively short life, the Pennydarren Tramway has an enduring claim to fame in that, in 1804, it was the venue for the first run of a steam locomotive on rails. On 21 February that year, an engine designed by the Cornishman Richard Trevithick successfully hauled five wagons loaded with pig-iron (and seventy men who had climbed aboard) from Merthyr to Abercynon. The weight of the locomotive broke many of the cast-iron rails and it had to be hauled back to Merthyr by a team of horses, but Trevithick did demonstrate that the idea was feasible. It would be for the Stephensons and others to turn this pioneering enterprise into a transport revolution.

D. The Alexandra (Newport & South Wales) Docks & Railway
This was a wonderfully eccentric railway, little known outside South Wales, which distinguished itself by providing passenger services in wild west saloons obtained from the circus train in which Buffalo Bill Cody toured the UK in the early years of this century. It started life as the Pontypridd, Caerphilly & Newport Railway, which was incorporated on 8 August 1878; it was nominally independent although backed by the Alexandra Dock Company of Newport, which viewed it as a means of increasing traffic to its dock.

Despite its prepossessing title, the PC&NR initially involved no new construction other than a 5¼ mile stretch between the south end of the Taff Vale Railway's station at Pontypridd and Penrhos Upper Junction, near Caerphilly. The rest of the journey was to be achieved by the exercise of running powers, a situation which caused the PC&NR and its successors to maintain unusually (one might almost say uniquely) good relations with their neighbours. The company's late arrival forced it to engineer a course fairly high up the east side of the Taff Vale, well away from the communities on the valley floor. The line was supposed to open on 7 July 1884, but the first trainload of coal got no further than Bassaleg on the Brecon & Merthyr Railway, where it was hoped that B&M running powers would enable it to continue its journey to Newport; however, the GWR signalman at Bassaleg Junction had other ideas and refused to let the train pass. It took eighteen days of negotiation before the situation was resolved: the line finally opened for goods on 25 July 1884, with passenger services commencing on 28 December 1887. Ten years later, the PC&NR was absorbed by the Alexandra Dock Company, which had changed its name in 1882 to the Alexandra (Newport & South Wales) Docks & Railway Company.

The line was conceived from the outset as a coal-carrying railway, but its first passenger services – far from being a poor relation – were expresses that ran from Pontypridd to Newport with only a single stop at Caerphilly.

The last days of the Alexandra (Newport & South Wales) Docks & Railway Company. It is June 1922 and a local train from Pontypridd Tram Road Halt to Caerphilly pulls into the passing loop at Rhydyfelin. A northbound train has just passed the other way, as revealed by the lowered signal arm. Note the station nameboard, the pedestrian crossing in the foreground and the solitary passenger standing on the 'platform' – a bed of cinders at rail level. The train itself is also of interest: the first coach is probably one of the company's two converted Drummond railmotors, while the second is a saloon car from Buffalo Bill Cody's circus train. The AD & R was 'grouped' into the GWR the following year

D.K. Jones

These were operated by the GWR from 1 January 1899 but were withdrawn by that company on 31 December 1916 as an economy measure. The Alexandra Docks & Railway began its own local services between Pontypridd and Caerphilly in April 1904 but, unwilling to pay the junction tolls demanded by the TVR for use of its Pontypridd station, constructed a new station of its own at Pontypridd Tram Road Halt. The words 'construct' and 'station' are a little extravagant here, while the appendage 'Tram Road Halt' gave intending passengers a clear indication of what to expect. This and a string of similar halts along the line consisted of little more than a gate in the boundary fence, a sprinkling of cinders beside the track, a wooden nameboard and an oil lamp for illumination. (In fact, the company could legitimately claim to have developed the prototype of the modern 'basic railway'!) The absence of any kind of platform meant that all passenger stock had to be fitted with steps so that passengers could board and alight, but fortunately Buffalo Bill's saloon cars, purchased in 1909, were already thus equipped.

This ramshackle passenger service survived until 17 September 1956, which seems little short of miraculous when one considers that many equivalent services – particularly those operated by Colonel Stephens, an inveterate collector of shoestring railways throughout the country – had closed in the 1930s. Doubtlessly they were subsidised by the line's profitable freight services, although these too were withdrawn on 31 July 1967.

E. The Rhymney Railway
At present, the Taff Trail uses only a short section of the Rhymney Railway between Nantgarw and Ty Rhiw. This was part of a line from Aber Junction (near Caerphilly) to Walnut Tree Junction (near Taff's Well), by which RR trains first travelled from Rhymney to Cardiff. It was authorized on 2 July 1855 and opened in 1858, for freight on 25 February and for passengers on 31 March. There were intermediate stations at Caerphilly and Taff's Well, although neither is shown on any of the currently available railway gazetteers.

While a perfectly reasonable route, the line was not a great success from an operational point of view because it necessitated running over the Taff Vale Railway between Walnut Tree Junction and Cardiff. Although the RR enjoyed running powers over this section, the TVR objected to its trains, which it claimed were overloaded, inadequately braked and hauled by under-powered engines. To add insult to injury, the TVR subjected RR trains to unpredictable delays and levied upon them an additional charge, which it had not agreed, of one old penny per ton.

The details of the resultant feud need not concern us here, but the Rhymney Railway quickly resolved that it needed to construct an independent route to Cardiff. It achieved this, at considerable expense, by burrowing beneath Cefn Onn mountain and approaching Cardiff from the north. This new line received its Act on 25 July 1864 but did not finally open until 1 April 1871. Very little published information is available on the original line to Walnut Tree Junction, but it seems safe to assume that its passenger services were withdrawn on the same date. Despite this, it continued to carry freight for more than a century until it was put out of use temporarily on 21 June 1982. It was reopened on 23 October that year to allow passage by a rail tour, but after that the only traffic was an occasional working at the Walnut Tree Junction end to a local contractors' yard. The line was closed permanently in March 1984; lifting started two months later and had been completed by March 1987.

F. The Barry Railway
If ever a railway had a bad press it was the Barry, which is frequently described as an 'octopus' with 'tentacles' reaching out from its coastal base to steal trade from other, longer established lines. Personally, I find this

somewhat unfair, for it gave access to a well-equipped modern dock and fulfilled a genuine role by relieving pressure on other harbours, such as Cardiff, which could ill cope with the volume of traffic descending on them.

The Barry Railway was a combined dock and railway company which, like several others in South Wales, was formed because the alternatives were not good enough and lacked the will to improve. The Bute Trustees, who controlled the docks at Cardiff, were particularly prone to this charge. Their operations were so inefficient that some local collieries had to suspend production because their every wagon was ensnared in the docks. The new company was first formed as the Barry Dock & Railway in 1865, but due to the poor financial climate at the time, no construction took place and its powers were formally abandoned in 1878–9. It was reincorporated on 14 August 1884, after which construction took place rapidly. The culmination of various local openings came on 18 July 1889, when the company opened Barry Dock and a connecting main line to Trehafod on the Taff Vale Railway. Having established the dock, it then set about expanding in every direction possible in order to ensure that it was well supplied with traffic.

The section of track now used by the Taff Trail is a case in point. It was authorized by an Act dated 7 August 1896, which granted powers for a line from Tyn-y-Caeau Junction (near Wenvoe) to Penrhos Upper Junction (near Caerphilly). The fact that earlier railways had claimed all the best ground made the engineering on this route difficult, as witnessed by the massive Walnut Tree Viaduct; this was 1,548 ft long, 120 ft high and crossed the Taff Vale by seven lattice girder spans. The line opened to goods and mineral traffic on 1 August 1901. Summer-only passenger services were inaugurated as an afterthought in 1924 but were withdrawn in 1932, although summer excursions continued via this route until 1964. However, the line's main purpose was to convey freight to Barry Dock, a task it performed extremely well. At its peak, eighty to ninety loaded coal trains from the Rhymney Valley were booked over this route every day, with similar traffic levels on other feeders to the dock as well. Despite claims that it was a parasite, the Barry Railway carried 3 million tons of coal in its first year (1889–90), rising to 11 million tons by 1913. These figures make it hard to deny that it was fulfilling a genuine need.

Goods services between Tyn-y-Caeau and Penrhos Upper junctions were withdrawn on 17 June 1963 with coal traffic following on 18 December 1967. Walnut Tree Viaduct, the line's principal landmark, was subsequently dismantled for scrap.

G. The Melingriffith Tramway

The Harford family of Melingriffith was responsible for the construction of this line, which was built in about 1815 to convey iron ore from quarries east of Pentyrch to their tinplate works near Whitchurch. The line was only 2 miles long and remained privately owned throughout its existence. However, it carried enough traffic to warrant rebuilding as a light railway and continued in use until about 1959.

Despite its relative obscurity, the Melingriffith Tramway possessed two features of outstanding interest for so small a line. The first was a level-crossing near Morganstown by which it traversed all four lines of the Taff Vale Railway's trunk route from Cardiff to Pontypridd. The second, less than a quarter of a mile to the south, was a bridge which carried it from the west to the east bank of the River Taff. The level-crossing was dismantled in 1962 but the bridge remains in place to this day; it now carries a public footpath.

The Lines Today

All of the above lines, to a greater or lesser extent, have been incorporated in the Taff Trail, together with sections of the Monmouthshire & Brecon Canal and the long-abandoned Glamorganshire Canal. The trail itself was developed between 1988 and 1993 as a long-distance cycle trail linking Brecon and Cardiff. The principal agency in its development was the Merthyr and Cynon Groundwork Trust, which co-ordinated over thirty private companies, local authorities and other public bodies involved in its construction. Such a large project inevitably has its problems; not every local authority was wholeheartedly in support of the scheme and this has led to some sections following a less than ideal route. Elsewhere, local difficulties have been resolved, temporarily at least, by devising two or more alternative routes between the same two places – an arrangement which leads to confusion in both marketing and using the trail.

However, there is far more to applaud than criticize in the project, not least the fact that the local Groundwork Trust is still striving to improve the trail and negotiate alternative routes where these are most needed. It is particularly creditable that so much of the trail is 'off road', i.e. entirely free from motorized traffic, while the reuse of various old tramways, railways and canals has created some excellent opportunities for those interested in industrial archaeology. Indeed, it is possible that the coming years will witness an increase in the mileage of disused industrial routes utilized in the trail as it is developed further.

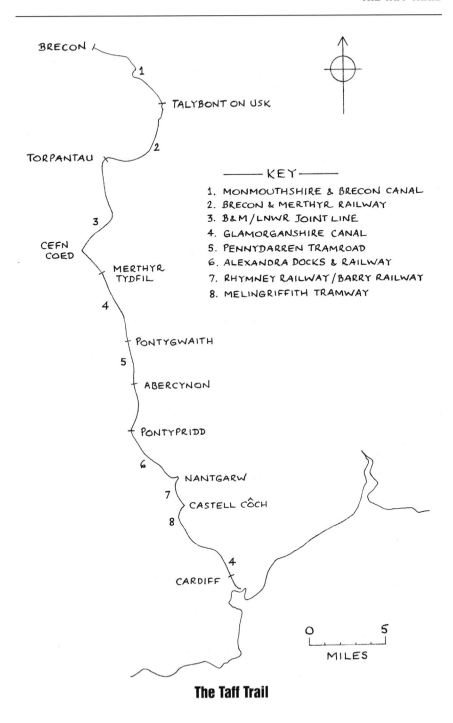

The Taff Trail

The Walk (52 Miles)

Note: Due to the exceptional length of this route, this account has been divided into sections corresponding to those used in *The Taff Trail Official Guide* (see Bibliography). As this is primarily a book on walking disused railways, those parts of the trail which utilize canals, riverside paths, minor roads, etc. are not described in detail and you are advised to follow local waymarking. Also, please remember that the trail is still being developed, which means that you may encounter alterations to the route described.

Brecon to Talybont-on-Usk (7 Miles)

The official Taff Trail map for this section indicates that there is a choice of routes here: one for cyclists based largely on the B4558 Brecon–Talybont

Not a railway walk, obviously, but a lovely evocation of a water-borne holiday on the Monmouthshire & Brecon Canal, whose towpath the Taff Trail follows between Brecon and Talybont-on-Usk. The boat has just passed under Twm Bridge, east of Brynich Aqueduct
John Gibberd

road, and the other for walkers based on the minor lanes around Llanfrynach. My advice is to ignore them both and use instead the towpath of the Monmouthshire & Brecon Canal which is traffic-free and far more interesting. Be warned, however, that it can be muddy in winter, while some cyclists find it rather overgrown in summer (I didn't myself, but I suspect that I have been inured by regularly cycling down abandoned railways). While on the subject of cycling, riders should obtain permission for their journey from the British Waterways office at Govilon (see Appendix A); they are unlikely to be refused unless they are part of a large group.

Starting in Brecon then, take the B4601 east from the town centre. Look out for Rich Way on the right-hand side, which is signposted to the canal wharf. At the end of Rich Way, turn left into Canal Road, and the wharf (such as it is) cannot be missed. The usual canal basin is completely missing in Brecon, having been filled in and redeveloped. The canal just starts from nothing on the east side of bridge No. 167. The canal towpath is extremely easy to follow, and traffic noise from the nearby B4601 reminds one what a wise decision it was to follow this route. The first lock, one of only six on the entire canal, is passed at Brynich (GR 077273). The canal then swings sharply to the south to cross Brynich Aqueduct, which carries the waterway across the fast-flowing River Usk. Another, smaller aqueduct follows 1½ miles later near Llanfrynach (GR 084257).

The winding and secluded course of the canal should be followed past Pencelli, where the Royal Oak offers a handy refreshment stop, to Talybont-on-Usk, which is heralded by a succession of lift bridges. There are two more pubs in Talybont, as well as shops and a café situated in the post office. Here, the Taff Trail leaves the canal via a 90 degree turn to the right. This is directly behind the White Hart pub and is very easy to find (GR 115225).

Talybont-on-Usk to Merthyr Tydfil (17 Miles)

It is tempting to pick up the course of the Brecon & Merthyr Railway at this point, but a red waymarking symbol indicates that this is not the route. Instead, walkers should follow the course of the old Brynoer Tramway, which crosses the railway by an overbridge at GR 114224. Modern red and white signs, complete with a weight restriction, declare that BR is still responsible for maintaining this bridge, even though it is over 10 miles from the nearest operational line.

After a zigzag to negotiate the bridge, the Brynoer Tramway begins its long climb up the side of Tor y Foel. At GR 108213, a clearing is reached with a new forest track running diagonally across the course of the tramway. This should be followed to the right, and the B&M trackbed will be reached at the foot of the hill (GR 108210). If you wish to follow the Taff Trail, don't do as I did and miss the turning; I came out at the top of the mountain at Pen Rhiw-calch, a further 3½ miles up the line. Having said this, the Brynoer Tramway is not without interest. Plenty of stone sleepers remain, complete with the impressions of rails and chairs, while at Pen Rhiw-calch, a shallow cutting remains which leads to an infilled under-bridge. If you have time to spare, the tramway can be followed for a further 3 miles to Ffos y Wern (GR 108152), where the trackbed has been taken over by a minor road. This can be followed for ½ mile to GR 114146, where the tramway forks off again on the left before reaching Trefil Limestone Quarries (GR 120133), which provided the primitive trains with some of their payload. The whole of the section from Talybont to Ffos y Wern is a bridleway, and the views above Pen Rhiw-calch are impressive.

Back on the B&M, the Taff Trail begins a long uphill climb which is only marginally less tiring than that up the Brynoer Tramway. At GR 107204, the line passes the dam at the north end of Talybont Reservoir, continuing past a Royal Navy centre (GR 103185) before reaching the site of Pentir Rhiw Halt (GR 102184). Never a busy station, Pentir Rhiw became even more quiet and lonely when the construction of Talybont Reservoir in the 1930s submerged the few farms it once served. At the end, the only passengers were hikers who purchased their tickets from the signalman.

Clearings in the surrounding forest are reached at GR 084169 and 071164. These provide the first opportunity to see how far the line has risen, and most walkers will be surprised at the sight of Talybont Reservoir in the distance, several miles away and over 350 ft below. Still the line climbs, curving around the contours to the west and north-west. At GR 057171, the trackbed becomes peculiarly cold and damp due to the proximity of Torpantau Tunnel, which houses the summit of the line. Here path and railway diverge, with the tunnel portal lying just off the trail to the left. The trackbed through the tunnel was very wet, even on a hot August day, and the portal had been bricked up, although – as usual – the door had been forced open. As the tunnel is on a curve, it is pitch black inside with not even the faintest glimmer of light from the other end. I peered into the inky darkness and proceeded via the official route.

The Taff Trail now climbs steeply uphill to join a minor road at GR 055175. On reaching this road, the walker should turn left and proceed uphill to the summit of the mountain. After a short distance, the official trail turns right for a scenic detour through Taf Fechan Forest. However, cyclists and those interested in tracing the old railway will probably prefer to keep to the road, which proceeds south past Pentwyn and Pontsticill reservoirs. This route passes a small car park along the west bank of Pontsticill Reservoir, where an ice-cream van can sometimes be found in the summer – a welcome facility after the long climb to Torpantau Tunnel. Further south, the Brecon Mountain Railway can be viewed on the far side of the reservoir. This narrow gauge line currently runs between Pant and Ponsticill stations, a distance of just under 2 miles.

At GR 057120, our short cut rejoins the Taff Trail and the official waymarking can then be followed across Pontsticill Dam to GR 061105, where the trail regains the trackbed. Pontsticill station lies 1 mile to the north of this point and it was here that the B&M diverged. The two lines continued southwards for just over a mile, running parallel along the western edge of Merthyr Common before the main line to Dowlais Top curved off to the south-east and the Merthyr branch to the south-west. The trail now follows the course of the latter, which from Morlais Junction was run jointly with the London & North Western Railway.

From here to Merthyr, it is downhill all the way. The line passes over the magnificent seven-arch Pontsarn Viaduct at GR 045099, with Taf Fechan far below. The south parapet of the viaduct faces the ruins of Morlais Castle, built on the summit of Morlais Hill in the thirteenth century to guard the mountain route to the Marcher Lordship of Glamorgan. The single platform of lonely Pontsarn station is passed shortly afterwards. The line continues to fall, with Taf Fechan to the left, until it reaches the village of Cefn Coed, now part of the Merthyr Tydfil conurbation. The route crosses the A465 by a girder bridge at GR 033081 before joining a narrow lane which comes out in Cefn Coed High Street (GR 032080), opposite the Railway Inn.

Cefn Coed station once stood on the opposite side of the road (GR 031079), and if further evidence were needed, the Station Hotel can be glimpsed over the rooftops. It is not currently part of the route, but if you have time, cross the road, pass the Station Hotel and walk south for about 200 yd past some rather bland 1960s flats. You will then find yourself at the north end of Cefn Coed Viaduct (GR 031078), the largest on the line and the third largest in Wales. The Merthyr and Cynon Groundwork Trust wants to divert the Taff Trail over this section of line, but the trackbed is currently blighted by a scheme for a new Merthyr Tydfil bypass which, at the very least, will cross the line south of here.

On reaching Cefn Coed, the Taff Trail leaves the course of the old railway and runs downhill along the High Street, now part of the A470. From here to Merthyr, it is best to rely on the waymarking, which is by a series of brown metal signs. One compelling reason for using the waymarking is that the route is still changing as new sections are developed.

Merthyr Tydfil to Pontypridd (13 Miles)

The trail leaves Merthyr Tydfil by the town's technical college (GR 046062) behind which is situated Ynysfach Engine House, an 1836 rebuild of an earlier structure, designed to pump air into the adjoining blast furnaces. The building has been lovingly restored and is open seven days a week (the hours vary according to the day and season, but it is always open between 2.00 and 4.00 p.m.). From here to Pont-y-Gwaith (GR 080976), the route follows a 6 mile section of the Glamorganshire Canal, built between 1790 and 1794. The towpath has been turned into a metre-wide cyclepath, but the shallow bed of the canal is frequently evident on the west side. Little remains of the canal structures, although a single canal bridge survives at GR 079976 (just south of Pont-y-Gwaith) and it is possible to imagine the site of locks where the path falls. At the Merthyr end, the towpath passes under a pair of disused railway lines, these being the Great Western branch from Merthyr to Neath, and the Great Western and Rhymney Railway joint line from Merthyr to Quaker's Yard. The latter can often be seen from the trail, just to the east and below it on the side of the valley.

At Pont-y-Gwaith (GR 080976), the path leaves the Glamorganshire Canal and runs east via the parish road to pick up the course of the Pennydarren Tramway, which is met by an impressive tramway bridge at GR 081978. The 3 mile section that follows is one of the loveliest, and most historic, on the whole of the Taff Trail. Much of the route lies beneath a canopy of broadleaved trees which provide some glorious colours in autumn, while on the ground, the stone tramway sleepers are still in place, complete with passing loops. Better things are yet to come, for between Edwardsville and Quaker's Yard, the line crosses the River Taff by a pair of single span stone bridges (GR 090965 and 094963), which were built in 1815 to replace their timber predecessors. (These improvements were forced on the company when the original bridge at Edwardsville collapsed with a train on it.) The route finishes in Tramroadside, Abercynon, which comes out by the town's fire station (GR 085949), built on the site of the former canal basin. Evidence of the past lies all around: the Navigation public house used to be the canal company's headquarters, while the nearby road bridge over the River Taff is built on top of Abercynon Aqueduct. Finally, a plaque outside the fire station commemorates the historic run of Trevithick's steam engine in 1804.

Between Abercynon and Pontypridd, the Taff Trail follows a mixture of roads and riverside paths – not a particularly good route, but at least it's only 3 miles long. The main features of transport interest, the Glamorganshire Canal and the Taff Vale Railway's branch from Pontypridd to Nelson, have largely been buried beneath the modern A470 dual carriageway.

This striking view of Pontsarn Viaduct near Merthyr Tydfil gives a clear impression of its grandeur. It is 455 ft long, 92 ft high and crosses the valley of the Taf Fechan by seven spans of 40 ft 6 in. It was reopened in July 1991 by Prince Charles after restoration as part of the Taff Trail

Once part of the Penllwyn Tramway, this imposing bridge near Nine Mile Point was strengthened some time after 1902 to take coal trains from a new colliery on the east side of the river. The brick reinforcements inside the original stone arch can be clearly seen. Nowadays, it has to take no more than the weight of passing walkers

David James Photography (Sussex)

Pontypridd to Castell Coch (8 Miles)

The Taff Trail leaves Pontypridd via Ynysangharad Road, which starts at GR 076904 from a horribly busy roundabout beneath the A470. Ynysangharad Road is notable for two reasons: firstly, the Glamorganshire Canal lies behind the houses on its south side, and secondly, it includes an excellent pub – the Bunch of Grapes. Hungry and thirsty travellers who stop off here will not be disappointed, for it offers a wide range of ales and plenty of good value bar snacks. The patio garden at the back overlooks the site of a staircase lock, followed by a lock keeper's cottage (recently restored), a still-extant canal bridge and the reed-filled basin which once served the works of Brown-Lenox Ltd., formerly a world-famous chain-making company.

Beyond the pub, it is another ¾ mile to Glyntaff, where the trail resumes its off-road course from a narrow alley-way off Cemetery Road (GR

Walkers following the Taff Trail south through Trallwng on the outskirts of Pontypridd will appreciate the view of this bridge on the former branch line from Pontypridd to Nelson. The coping stone on the central pier is clearly marked with the initials of the Taff Vale Railway, which opened this end of the route in 1887. The line closed to passengers in 1932 and to freight in 1949

Author

087892). This unprepossessing start leads to the trackbed of the former Alexandra (Newport & South Wales) Docks & Railway Company, which is now followed for the next 3½ miles to Nantgarw. In years gone by, this part of the valley must have been an interesting place for railway enthusiasts, as no less than five separate railways converged here. On the far west lay the Taff Vale line from Llantrisant, followed closely by the Barry Railway's main line from Cadoxton. Next came the Taff Vale's line from Cardiff to Merthyr – the only one open to this day – followed by the ill-fated Cardiff Railway (Heath Junction to Treforest) and, high up the eastern slopes of the valley, our own line to Caerphilly. Trail users may wonder why this route gains height when it is actually proceeding southwards down the valley; the explanation lies in the fact that it is climbing out of the Taff Vale to cross the hills preceding Caerphilly.

Given the proximity of so much housing and industry, this old railway has a surprisingly silvan look about it – proof, were it needed, that disused

This is the site of Upper Boat Halt on the Alexandra Docks & Railway Company's line between Pontypridd and Penrhos Junction near Caerphilly. Nothing remains of the primitive station, which is hardly surprising considering that it was little more than a bed of cinders at rail level. Once an important coal-carrying line, the route is remarkable now for its rustic appearance in what – on the valley floor at least – is still a busy and urban area

John Gibberd

trackbeds make marvellous 'green arteries' in urban areas. The line alternates between enclosed and open sections, the latter giving a bird's-eye view over the valley. One notable feature is the blackness of the open spaces in Treforest Industrial Estate, which reveals the former influence of coal mining. Practically nothing remains of the wayside halts along the line, although their locations can be guessed at from the proximity of bridges and local lanes.

At Nantgarw, the trail turns sharply to the right and makes its way to the A468, which it crosses by a pelican crossing at GR 127857. On the south side of the road, the trail descends to pick up fragments of two more railways, these being the Rhymney Railway's line from Caerphilly to Taff's Well, and the Barry Railway's Rhymney branch. The Rhymney Railway is joined first but is abandoned after barely a mile in favour of the Barry line, which skirts around the village of Ty Rhiw. Just beyond Ty Rhiw, the trail switches to a forest path which climbs steeply to reach Castell Coch (GR 131827), a Victorian fantasy castle built in the 1870s by the 3rd Marquis of Bute and his architect, William Burges. (The final approach to the castle

Between Nantgarw and Ty Rhiw, the Taff Trail switches from the Rhymney Railway to the Barry Railway at a point where their trackbeds run parallel. If you have cycled all the way from Brecon, the short connecting slope seems quite formidable!

John Gibberd

involves an even steeper descent, for which cyclists are urged to dismount.) The rest of the Barry's line to Walnut Tree Viaduct and beyond lies abandoned and overgrown, and cannot be used anyway as it finishes half way up a hillside now that the viaduct has been demolished.

Castell Coch to Cardiff Castle (7 Miles)

South of Castell Coch, the trail runs through the village of Tongwynlais before picking up the course of the Melingriffith Tramway. To reach this, leave the castle by the main drive and turn right at the end into Castle Road (GR 134827). Proceed downhill to a T junction with the A4054, Merthyr Road (GR 133823), and turn left. Follow Merthyr Road south as far as the Victorian school on the right at GR 135821 and there turn right into Iron Bridge Road. Follow this under the M4, turning immediately right then left after the motorway bridge, and continue as far as the river bank at GR 132816. You will then be standing on the course of the Melingriffith Tramway. The nearby river bridge carrying the public footpath to Morganstown was part of the line also, although the footpath leaves the trackbed on reaching the western bank. North-west of the bridge after about 300 yd the tramway crossed the TVR main line via a skew level crossing which cut across all four running lines. All this is now private land.

The tramway may be followed south for just under 2 miles to Melingriffith on the edge of Whitchurch. In places, the formation is still very clear but modern housing developments at the southern end have paid little respect to history. Although a right of way has been preserved, it is surfaced entirely in modern materials and gives no clue as to its origins. The tramway originally ended at GR 143801, where the Harford family's tinplate works once stood. The Harfords would hardly recognize the area today as it has been redeveloped with executive-style housing, but they would be familiar with the famous Melingriffith water pump which survives at GR 142799. This was installed shortly after 1806 at the suggestion of John Rennie. It was used to pump water which had passed through the tinplate works back into the Glamorganshire Canal, and was intended as a means of relieving water shortages in the section between here and Cardiff. As a matter of interest, a restored section of the canal – including the only surviving lock at GR 137809 – is situated nearby; this is now managed as a nature reserve by the Cardiff Naturalists' Society.

From here on, no more is seen of disused railways although the trail makes extensive use of the Glamorganshire Canal between Melingriffith and Cardiff Castle – not that one would recognize it as a canal nowadays. However, you'll know what you're travelling on when you pass the back of the Canal Boat public house in North Road, Cardiff. Why not pop in for a pint of Brains beer? If you've come all the way from Brecon, as I had, you'll have earned it!

Further Explorations

I find it hard to believe that anyone who has just explored the whole length of the Taff Trail could possibly want more industrial walking and cycling, but there is plenty to be had. Starting at the northern end, the towpath of the Monmouthshire & Brecon Canal can be followed to Pontypool and, even after that, much of it survives all the way to Newport. (The local authorities have recently upgraded parts of this section, as described in Chapter 11.) The Brynoer Tramway offers another substantial walk, with 9½ miles of trackbed surviving from Talybont-on-Usk to Trefil Limestone Quarries at the head of the Sirhowy Valley.

In the Merthyr Tydfil area, there are two shorter possibilities. The Dare Valley Country Park, just over a mile west of Aberdare, offers nearly 5 miles of railway walks, while the western branch of the Taff Trail (which travels from Brecon to Merthyr via Storey Arms) takes in sections of the old navvies' line which was laid in the closing years of the last century to help build the three reservoirs which now lie on the western side of the A470 Brecon–Merthyr road. Much of this can be walked by following the Taff Trail waymarking between Cantref and Llwyn-On reservoirs, but the fact that the trackbed beside Llwyn-On reservoir has been tarmacked makes it difficult to recognize as a disused railway.

Finally, South Glamorgan County Council has created a number of cycleways other than the Taff Trail, including a network of routes in the Penarth and Sully area. While none of these utilize disused railway lines, they offer some pleasant journeys through local countryside and along the coast. The main entrance to this network is at GR 180693 near Cosmeston Lakes Country Park, just south of Penarth on the B4267.

Transport and Facilities

Maps: Ordnance Survey: Landranger Series Sheets 160, 161, 170, 171
          Outdoor Leisure Map 11
          Pathfinder Series Sheets 1109, 1129, 1148, 1165

Taff Trail Project: Taff Trail Sectional Route Maps: Set of 6, free of charge from Merthyr & Cynon Groundwork Trust, Fedw Hir, Llwydcoed, Aberdare, Mid Glamorgan, CF44 0DX
Telephone: Aberdare (0685) 883880

Buses: Parfitts Motor Services, Llechryd Garage,
Rhymney Bridge, Gwent, NP2 5QD
Telephone: Rhymney (0685) 840329
Services: Merthyr Tydfil–Ponsticill

Red & White, Gadlys, Aberdare, CF44 8DH
Telephone: Aberdare (0685) 881888
Services: Merthyr Tydfil–Pontsticill
         Brecon–Talybont–Abergavenny–Newport

Silverline Coaches (National Express),
5 Beechwood Drive, Heolgerrig, Merthyr Tydfil, CF48 1ST
Telephone: Merthyr Tydfil (0685) 382406
Services: Merthyr Tydfil–Storey Arms–Brecon

Mid Glamorgan County Council, Public Transport Group,
Highways & Transportation Department,
Greyfriars Road, Cardiff, CF1 3LG
Telephone: Cardiff (0222) 820626 (direct line)

Powys County Council, Highways & Transportation,
County Hall, Llandrindod Wells, Powys, LD1 5LG
Telephone: Llandrindod Wells (0597) 826643

South Glamorgan County Council,
Highway & Transportation Services, County Hall,
Atlantic Wharf, Cardiff, CF1 5UW
Telephone: Cardiff (0222) 873252 (direct line)

Trains: British Rail Telephone Enquiry Bureau
Telephone: Cardiff (0222) 228000

Cycle Hire: Taff Trail Cycle Hire, Forest Farm Country Park,
Whitchurch, Cardiff
Telephone: Cardiff (0222) 751235

Taff Trail Cycle Hire is open daily during school holidays and every Saturday, Sunday and Bank Holiday from Easter to October. Opening hours: 10 a.m. to 6 p.m. Hire charges from £3.50.

Given the length of the Taff Trail, it is only possible to provide a thumbnail sketch of public transport in the limited space available here; a comprehensive summary of services appears in *The Taff Trail Official Guide* (see Bibliography). Basically, a split occurs at Merthyr Tydfil, with excellent services to the south (including a BR branch line to Cardiff) and relatively thin services to the north. Unless you are travelling on a Sunday, when some forward planning is required, you can take it for granted that a bus route accompanies the Merthyr – Cardiff section of the trail with a service running at least once an hour; the fact that several run every 15, 20 or 30 minutes will come as a pleasant surprise.

North of Merthyr, everything thins out – to the point of extinction on Sundays – and forward planning is essential. There is a bus every two hours from Merthyr to Pontsticill, but nothing between Pontsticill and Talybont-on-Usk. At Talybont, there is a bus approximately every two hours into Brecon. The only other useful service is the Silverline Coach from Merthyr Tydfil to Brecon, which connects with certain BR trains at Merthyr station. Unfortunately, this runs via the A470 and rarely comes within 5 miles of the route described in this chapter. Having said this, it is ideal if you are planning to walk back from Brecon to Merthyr, but at 24 miles the distance involved is on the high side.

Pubs are easily found except between Talybont and Pontsticill – no brewer thought to construct a tavern for the benefit of railway staff whose lot it was to work at the lonely and frequently frozen summit station of Torpantau. Be warned, however, that some of the pubs are fairly basic, both in and outside the towns. Shops and other facilities are close to the trail at Brecon, Talybont, Cefn Coed, Merthyr Tydfil, Quaker's Yard, Abercynon, Pontypridd, Tongwynlais and Cardiff.

10
THE DARRAN VALLEY
Parc Cwm Darran to Bargoed

Introduction

The modern cycle trail from Parc Cwm Darran to Bargoed was once part of a through route from Brecon to Newport used by trains of the Brecon & Merthyr Tydfil Junction Railway, whose northern section we examined in some detail in the previous chapter. However, while the views from the famous Seven Mile Bank between Torpantau and Talybont-on-Usk have been blotted out by modern forestry, no such obstruction exists in the Darran Valley. The views here are vast and wild, dominated at the northern end by a series of three new lakes which offer some of the finest coarse fishing in South Wales.

Parc Cwm Darran, where the trail starts, was created in the late 1970s from the remains of Olgivie Colliery, although few would imagine this today were it not for an old pit-head wheel and several jet black colliery trams left in evidence. The project as a whole has been remarkably successful, attracting large numbers of visitors and winning a Civic Trust Award in 1990. Not content to let matters rest, the two councils involved – Mid Glamorgan County and Rhymney Valley District – have continued to invest large sums of money, culminating in the opening of an impressive new visitor centre in 1994. They have also extended the project's brief far beyond the park itself, as witnesses the revival of the old railway. Any miner returning to Olgivie Colliery after an absence of twenty years or more would scarcely believe his eyes.

History

The Brecon & Merthyr Railway's intention of penetrating southwards was advertised in its first bill, published on 9 November 1858. Apart from the

Brecon–Dowlais main line, this proposed two branches of 4½ miles each. The first of these would run from Dowlais into the Bargoed Rhymney (or Darran) Valley, there connecting with an as yet unbuilt extension from the Rhymney Railway's main line at Bargoed. The second would push eastwards from Dowlais Top over the moors to Rhymney where it would connect with the 'old' Rumney Railway, a 22 mile tramroad that reached down to Bassaleg on the Monmouthshire Railway. However, as the bill progressed, the proposals for both of these branches disappeared, apparently in response to objections from the Rhymney Iron Company which feared interference with its operations.

Undeterred, the B&M returned to Parliament in 1861 with a renewed proposal for a branch into the Bargoed Rhymney Valley. This triggered a long dispute with the Rhymney Railway, which had obtained powers for such a line in 1854 but had never exercised them. The RR responded by reviving its earlier scheme, which Parliament duly sanctioned – along with the rival B&M bill which was enacted on the same day, 6 August 1861. The resultant battle has been described as 'one of the minor classics of Victorian railway history'.

The basic problems were twofold: firstly, the southern end of the valley was so narrow that only a single railway could be accommodated; and secondly, the two antagonists were so intent on destructive rivalry that they failed to appreciate fully the two and a half pages of mutually restrictive clauses that Parliament had written into their respective Acts. At one time, the valley between Groesfaen and Bargoed was staked out with two sets of surveyors' pegs, one overlapping the other! It was two years before the antagonists came to their senses and devised a compromise, whereby the B&M built the section from Dowlais to Deri Junction, and the RR the remainder from Deri Junction to Bargoed. The B&M was given running powers for through traffic, in return for which the RR was allowed to work coal traffic to Pantywaen Junction near Dowlais, although it only exercised these rights as far as the collieries at Fochriw.

The section south of Deri Junction was brought into use in March 1864, but although the B&M completed the link from Dowlais to Deri the following year, it was unable to run any trains over it for another three years. This was the result of legal complications connected to its Act of 1861. The problem with devising plans for expansion in every direction was that the B&M made many enemies, including the Taff Vale Railway which had Parliament add a clause to this Act forbidding use of the line in the Bargoed Rhymney Valley until it had completed its branch from Pontsticill to Merthyr Tydfil.

This project was uppermost in the minds of the B&M directors when on 'Black Friday', 10 May 1866, the company's bankers, Overend & Gurney, collapsed with debts of over £11 million. Work on the Merthyr branch

This is the coal preparation plant at Groesfaen Colliery, photographed in June 1969. Note the platforms of the adjoining halt and the double track, still in good condition despite the withdrawal of passenger and freight facilities in 1962 and 1965 respectively. Only a single platform remains today, and the colliery has been reduced to a green meadow where crickets chirp in the afternoon sun

Powys County Museum Service (Welsh Industrial & Maritime Museum)

ceased immediately and, later the same year, the B&M went into receivership, unable to pay its creditors or the interest due on its debenture shares. The company remained in the hands of the Official Receiver until 1868, when its debts were restructured as extra debenture shares. Two years later, the court ratified an arrangement with its creditors which provided, *inter alia*, that no legal action was to be taken against the company for ten years without the court's express permission. While all this was going on, Alexander Sutherland, the B&M engineer, struggled against the odds to complete the Merthyr branch, which finally opened throughout on 1 August 1868. This removed the constraint on the line in the Bargoed Rhymney Valley, which opened to passengers exactly a month later on 1 September.

In order to explain the importance of this opening, it is necessary to go back to 1861 and the 'old' Rumney Railway. In this year, the old Rumney obtained an Act which reincorporated it as a proper railway and authorized various improvements, most of which it was too poor to implement. The Act also allowed for its purchase by either the Monmouthshire or West

Midland Railway, but when neither of these companies moved to acquire it, the B&M stepped in. Its take-over was authorized by an Act dated 28 July 1863, which rather generously fixed the price of the old Rumney at a maximum of £90,000 – an acknowledgement that few of the intended improvements had actually taken place. At the southern end of its line, the old Rumney enjoyed running powers over GWR metals from Bassaleg Junction to Newport, which neatly fulfilled the B&M's ambition of reaching the Bristol Channel.

The consequence of all this was that, when the line through Deri Junction opened in 1868, the passenger trains were not just locals but long distance services between Brecon and Newport. There were initially three of these workings per day, running through to Newport (Dock Street). They were diverted to Newport (High Street), the GWR station, on 11 March 1880 when that company opened a new link to its South Wales main line between Park Junction and Gaer Junction. The total distance from Brecon to Newport was 47 miles. The best ever journey time was achieved in the summer of 1914 with a booked working of 2 hours and 18 minutes, although less favoured services took nearly 3 hours. In the late 1950s, the journey time was about 2½ hours, which was not bad considering the mountainous terrain and the fact that the trains observed no less than twenty-two intermediate stops.

But all this is to jump ahead somewhat, for the story of railways in the Bargoed Rhymney Valley is not quite finished. The last proposal for a new line in the area came in 1905, when the Barry Railway (which by this time had already tapped B&M traffic at Duffryn Isaf, north-west of Bedwas) fought vigorously to obtain its own line between Aberbargoed and Deri Junction. The proposed route has all the characteristics of a typical Barry line, for as usual, earlier companies had secured all the best ground. The new construction was intended to leave the old Rumney line at Aberbargoed and cross the Rhymney Railway's main line north of Bargoed; it would then plunge into a 220 yd tunnel, thereby avoiding the narrowest section of the valley between Bargoed and Groesfaen. Finally, it would join the B&M north of Deri Junction, offering a route which entirely avoided use of running powers over the Rhymney Railway. If this was an attempt to court the B&M, it was unsuccessful, and the Barry Railway had many enemies besides; the scheme accordingly failed in 1906.

After the excitement of these early years, the rest of the line's history was fairly uneventful. The Brecon–Newport passenger service usually amounted to three or four return workings per day, augmented by a number of local journeys which covered part rather than the whole of the line. In July 1922, stations in the Bargoed Rhymney Valley enjoyed a service of five trains in each direction per day, augmented by two extra workings on Saturdays. These included the obligatory late night Saturday special, which presumably

An abandoned pithead wheel lies alongside the empty trackbed of the Brecon & Merthyr Railway at Parc Cwm Darran, formerly Ogilvie Colliery. Landscape artists have moved in where miners once toiled and the site is now unrecognisable as a former part of the South Wales industrial scene

David James Photography (Sussex)

carried wassailing miners from Bargoed back to their homes. In addition, a number of long distance holiday trains used the line, normally starting at Newport or Cardiff and running via Bargoed to the central Wales spa towns or Aberystwyth. As with many other railways, the public timetable told only part of the story, for the line was also busy with colliers' specials and heavily laden coal trains which had an easy job on the 1 in 40 gradient from Fochriw down to Bargoed North Junction. It was these services, running through to Newport, that made the real money on the Brecon & Merthyr. Had the company's board not included a number of prominent Brecon backers who obliged it to construct the mountainous northern section, it might have been a very profitable railway indeed.

After the turn of the century, traffic reached such a level that the Rhymney Railway doubled the section from Deri Junction to Bargoed in 1909, and the cost of this was undoubtedly met by profits from the South Wales coal trade. Although this peaked in 1913, it remained substantial for many years to come, particularly during World War I when a number of 'Jellicoe Specials' were routed over the B&M due to congestion on the more obvious routes to the north. (These trains conveyed supplies of coal to Scapa Flow, where Lord Jellicoe's fleet was based.)

On 1 July 1922, the B&M was absorbed by the GWR, which maintained the basic pattern of services but made its usual improvements to locomotives and rolling stock. A quarter of a century and another world war later, the line became part of the Western Region of British Railways on 1 January 1948. It is a credit to the B&M's locomotive builders that no less than thirteen of its engines survived into BR ownership, the last of these being BR numbers 1668 and 1670, which were withdrawn in February 1954.

The rest of the line's history is the usual tale of contraction and closure, brought about by the decline of the coal industry and competition from buses and private cars. Passenger services between Brecon and Newport were withdrawn on 31 December 1962 and, on this line at least, freight services did not last much longer. They were withdrawn between Pant and Deri Junction on 1 April 1963, and between Deri Junction and Bargoed on 23 August 1965.

The Line Today

The rails in the valley were lifted some time after June 1969, the trackbed remaining unused until the 1970s when it was purchased by Mid Glamorgan County Council, which financed the acquisition with a hundred per cent grant from the Welsh Development Agency for derelict land reclamation. At the same time, Olgivie and Groesfaen collieries with their attendant buildings and spoil heaps were subjected to extensive landscaping, which has left their sites unrecognizable – and massively improved. The construction of the cycle trail followed, with funds coming from a variety of sources including the WDA, the Countryside Commission and the local authorities.

In June 1989, Rhymney Valley District Council published its 'Countryside Recreation and Management Strategy', which promised the 'substantial definition and completion of a cycleway system for the County' within a period of five years. The Darran Valley route was seen as an important element in this system and the council proposed to extend it both north and southwards. Unfortunately, schemes like this have a tendency to run late – just like B&M passenger trains – especially at a time of prolonged economic recession. However, the extensions have not been abandoned and are reviewed briefly under 'Further Explorations'.

The Walk (4½ Miles)

The best place to access this walk is Parc Cwm Darran (GR 113035) on the minor road from Bargoed to Fochriw. Most walkers will be tempted immediately to head off south down the valley, but it is worth starting out in the opposite direction, for the trail extends a good half mile north towards Fochriw. Half way along, there is a wooden sign announcing the end of the cycle trail followed by a post and wire fence across the line, but a stile allows walkers to continue. The going is easy as far as a demolished bridge at GR 109043 where it is best to turn back, but before you do, have a look up and down the valley: the views are impressive. Fochriw is clearly visible to the north and the line marches off towards it as a grassy embankment grazed by

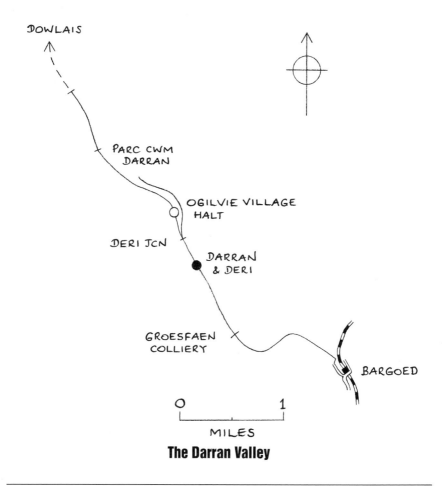

The Darran Valley

Parc Cwm Darran, complete with its three award winning lakes, is a modern phoenix that has risen from the ashes of Olgivie Colliery. Were proof needed, the site is dotted with colliery artefacts such as this old colliery tram

David James Photography (Sussex)

horses and geese. It is now over thirty years since the last train passed this way and it is astonishing that the railway formation has survived so completely intact.

Returning to the main park entrance, part of the trackbed is still ballasted which makes it hard going if you are on a bicycle. However, this is the exception rather than the rule, for the rest of the trail has a good, smooth surface. When I visited, an old pit-head wheel and colliery tram had been left by the side of the line as a reminder that the area was once dominated by Olgivie Colliery – the pit-head wheel had been painted electric blue, so there was no missing it. The area was restored in the 1970s when the three modern lakes, visible through the trees on the left, were created.

Continuing south, the site of Olgivie Village Halt is reached at GR 125026, although no trace remains of the old station. The small settlement includes a chapel and a useful pub, the Bargoed Inn. In years gone by, this was a busy place. The line from Bargoed was double track as far as the halt, but single track thereafter all the way to Pant. A quarter of a mile to the south, the branch to Olgivie Colliery came off on the east side at Deri Junction with both lines running up the valley on opposite sides of the river. The evidence of this is clearly visible at GR 125025 where a pair of

There isn't much to see of Olgivie Village Halt nowadays, but it was situated in the right foreground of this picture. The trackbed on the right once accommodated the Brecon & Merthyr line from Bassaleg to Pontsticill, while that on the left accommodated a short branch from Deri Junction to Olgivie Colliery. The timber bridges in the middle distance, so typical of B & M construction, are now listed buildings

David James Photography (Sussex)

antiquated wooden bridges cross the line, sometimes occupied by horses and donkeys which peer over the parapet wondering when the next train might come. Both bridges are now listed buildings, so their long-term future is assured. Incidentally, Deri Junction was a junction in name only, being merely an end-on connection between the systems of the two companies which built the line.

Darran and Deri station follows in ½ mile at GR 128018; this was situated immediately to the south of the now demolished rail-over-road bridge. A pub and general store are both close at hand if refreshments are required. Although the station has been demolished, its goods shed survives in a builder's yard on the left, while a solitary signal post sprouts from a large bush nearby on the right. Half a mile south of Darran and Deri, the empty trackbed passes the site of Groesfaen Colliery, which had buildings and sidings on both sides of the line. Although the colliery has been landscaped out of existence, a platform for the colliers' trains still survives, together with a pair of rails embedded in the remains of a concrete level crossing. All credit must go to the authorities who have restored this area, for the result is quite idyllic; but the remains of this platform, now surrounded by fields and the clicking of crickets, are inexplicable without a knowledge of local history.

Shortly after the colliery, the line begins to curve eastwards and passes over an attractive stone and brick bridge at GR 137004. This carries a small stream under the line, which is joined by a drainage channel from the nearby mountain – actually a landscaped spoil heap. Both watercourses are attractively edged with facing stones, which creates a sculptural effect reminiscent of water currents. The line then enters a particularly narrow and wooded section of the valley before curving south-eastwards for the final approach to Bargoed. Here at GR 146005, a footpath crosses the line by a delicate-looking metal bridge and, to my great surprise, I found that the span was still fitted with two steam deflectors to protect pedestrians from the exhaust of passing trains. One does not see many of these twenty-six years after the end of BR steam.

In another ¼ mile, the trackbed reaches a small open area (GR 149003) where the trail swings right and uphill to join a residential road leading to the A469 just south of Bargoed station (GR 151000). This diversion is necessary to prevent walkers and cyclists inadvertently alighting on BR's operational Rhymney Valley line (Bargoed North Junction was situated just outside the station at GR 150002). When you reach the main road, turn right for Bargoed town centre or left for the railway station. Whether you intend to catch a train or not, it is worth popping round to the station just to view the impressive viaduct which lies beyond. This was built in the mid 1850s and consists of seven spans rising to a height of nearly 70 ft above the valley floor.

The whole of this trail is a real delight with extensive views from beginning to end, and Mid Glamorgan County Council must be complimented on its work in restoring an industrial valley to its present verdant state. The landscaping of the 1970s has been so effective that it is difficult to imagine what the area must have looked like in the 1930s, when the collieries were in full production and trainloads of grimy colliers made the daily journey from Fochriw to Pengam in their antiquated 'colliers' specials'.

Further Explorations

At present, there is not a great deal more railway walking in the immediate vicinity although, to the south, a section of the Rhymney Railway's Senghenydd branch can be walked between Caerphilly and Abertridwr. This single track line was opened in 1894 to serve Windsor Colliery at the north end of the narrow, steep-sided valley leading to Senghenydd and closed with the colliery in 1977. (As a matter of interest, Windsor coal continued to be extracted but was carried underground to Nantgarw, about 4 miles to the south.)

In the longer term, Mid Glamorgan County Council proposes to extend the Darran Valley cycle route northwards to Merthyr Tydfil where it will join the Taff Trail (see Chapter 7), and southwards to Ystrad Mynach where it will connect with a route running from Quaker's Yard eastwards to Gelligroes and the Sirhowy Valley (see Chapter 11). As noted earlier, these developments are taking longer than expected to implement, but a footpath to Fochriw and a cycle trail to Ystrad Mynach are both possible by 1995; the latter depends on local land reclamation and the timetable for the Bargoed bypass. Further land reclamation east of Merthyr holds the key to the northern extension, but this is unlikely to be achieved before 1996.

At Caerphilly, the council also proposes to complete the 'Three Castles Cycle Route' by creating a link to Castell Coch along the Rhymney Railway's disused branch to Walnut Tree Junction. For many years, this route has only connected the castles at Castell Coch and Cardiff – two castles, not three.

Transport and Facilities

Maps: Ordnance Survey: Landranger Series Sheet 171
Ordnance Survey: Pathfinder Series Sheet 1109 (recommended)

Buses: Parfitts Motor Services, Llechryd Garage,
Rhymney Bridge, Gwent, NP2 5QD
Telephone: Rhymney (0685) 840329

Mid Glamorgan County Council, Public Transport Group,
Highways & Transportation Department,
Greyfriars Road, Cardiff, CF1 3LG
Telephone: Cardiff (0222) 820626 (direct line)

Trains: British Rail Telephone Enquiry Bureau
Telephone: Cardiff (0222) 228000

Bus services in the Darran Valley are excellent. Parfitts Motor Services provides a combined frequency of one bus every 20 minutes between Bargoed and Fochriw on routes P1 and P4 (the P1 runs to Pontlottyn or

Merthyr Tydfil, and the P4 to Abertysswg). During the evenings and Sunday afternoons, there is one bus per hour on route P4. There are no buses at all on Sunday mornings. Bargoed is also served by trains on British Rail's Rhymney Valley line. This has a half-hourly service on Mondays to Saturdays, with trains running every hour on weekday evenings and every two hours on Sunday afternoons from about 3 p.m.

On the refreshments side, the Visitor Centre at Parc Cwm Darran includes a useful café which is open from Easter to October, while backpackers and campers will appreciate the park's campsite. Pubs may be found at Olgivie Village (The Bargoed Inn), Deri (The Station Hotel) and Bargoed, where there is a wide choice, but once again large national brewers predominate. In years gone by, the local ale came from Rhymney Breweries Ltd., a business founded in 1836 by the Rhymney Iron Company which we met earlier. Whether the iron company was seeking to provide its workers with a quality product, or merely making a profit from their leisure as well as their labour will probably never be known. Whitbread & Co. acquired Rhymney Breweries in January 1966 and closed them down twelve years later as part of a devastating rationalization process which has only drawn to a close in recent years; but that is another story.

11
SIRHOWY VALLEY COUNTRY PARK

Crosskeys to Gelligroes

Introduction

Outside Wales, and possibly even South Wales at that, the Sirhowy Valley is little known. It is the next valley west from Ebbw Vale (the venue of the 1992 Garden Festival) and is dominated at the northern end by Tredegar, whose development is intricately linked with the railway line described in this chapter. The industrial development of the valley began in earnest at the start of the nineteenth century with the result that, by the mid 1820s, no less than three tramways had been constructed. These provided better transport than the primitive local roads with the Penllwyn Tramroad serving the southern end of the valley, Hall's Road the northern end, and the Sirhowy Tramroad its entire length.

Of these three, Hall's Road lasted the longest, being converted into a railway by the GWR and closing in 1989 along with Oakdale Colliery, the last of the many collieries it once served. It was constructed in 1805 by Benjamin Hall, whose son of the same name became Chief Commissioner of Works and achieved lasting fame by installing Big Ben at the Houses of Parliament. (Little known this valley may be, but one of its families still makes a daily contribution to the ITN News!)

History

The start of railways in the Sirhowy Valley can be traced to 20 March 1800, when Richard Fothergill, Matthew Monkhouse, Samuel Homfray and others signed a lease from Sir Charles Morgan for the use of rich mineral land about one mile south of Sirhowy – a site which later became famous as Tredegar Ironworks. At the time, iron from Dowlais and Merthyr was hauled to Newport by road in mule trains, but the new consortium wisely wanted better transport than this. Likewise, the Monmouthshire Canal Company, which already had an operational canal from Newport to Crumlin, was anxious to extend into the Sirhowy Valley in order to tap this potentially valuable new traffic.

The result of these rival interests was a compromise authorized by the Monmouthshire Canal Act of 26 June 1802. The canal company was empowered to build a tramroad from the River Usk at Newport to Nine Mile Point (so called because it was exactly nine miles from milepost zero), while the newly formed Sirhowy Tramroad Company would continue the line from Nine Mile Point to Sirhowy Furnaces. The tramroad was built rapidly and opened to goods and mineral traffic in 1805.

Horses initially supplied the motive power, with stables being provided at Tredegar, Rock, Nine Mile Point and Danycraig, near Risca. Wagons were restricted to a speed of 4 m.p.h. with a maximum laden weight of 56 cwt. and rather comically, the rule book insisted that no wagon should have less than four wheels. John Kingston of Newport introduced a passenger service in 1822, and about eight years later, the first steam locomotives were used. These were of a type similar to Stephenson's *Rocket* and proved about a third less expensive to operate than the horses. Despite this, horses continued to work on the line for a number of years, and the company whitewashed the fronts of its locomotives every week in order to make them conspicuous from a distance.

In 1855, the Monmouthshire line from Nine Mile Point to Newport was converted into a railway and this put pressure on the Sirhowy Tramroad Company to do the same. Unfortunately, conversion from a plateway using L shaped tramplates into a railway using edge rail and modern flanged wheels was very difficult because stock of both types was operated simultaneously. The company's solution was to lay special rails which accommodated both systems. These had inner tramplates of 4 ft 2 in gauge and outer edge rails of 4 ft 8 in gauge. This proved an effective solution until 25 May 1860, when the Sirhowy Railway Act authorized conversion of the tramroad into a standard gauge railway within a period of three years. During conversion, the company took the opportunity to make its route safer in places such as Tredegar, where the rails were moved from the streets to the backs of houses.

The next landmark in the company's history was a second Sirhowy Railway Act passed on 5 July 1865. This authorized an extension at the northern end from Sirhowy to Nantybwch (by which the London & North Western Railway would soon gain access to the line) and regularized the

Sirhowy–Newport passenger service which had started on 19 June of the same year. The 1860 Act had not envisaged through workings, so passengers from the upper part of the valley were expected to change trains at Nine Mile Point. This was regarded as inconvenient, with the result that the new Act provided for three through workings daily in each direction.

It is generally held that conversion into a railway drained the company's resources, for in 1874 it approached the Monmouthshire company and later the Great Western Railway with a view to selling out. However, these negotiations fell through with the result that the Monmouthshire company went to the GWR and the Sirhowy Railway to the rival LNWR. These arrangements were endorsed by an Act dated 13 July 1876. The LNWR was highly pleased with its acquisition, for the Sirhowy Railway and its running powers to Newport gave it what it had wanted for many years: access to the rich industrial valleys of South Wales and a major port on the Bristol Channel. Following the takeover, new buildings were installed at Nine Mile Point and Ynysddu, as well as elsewhere on the system; then in 1891, the whole of the line was doubled, completing a process which the Sirhowy Railway had started south of Tredegar in 1875.

Some of the halts on the Sirhowy Valley line are given away by narrow lanes that reach out to the railway from the far side of the valley. This is the site of Pont Lawrence Halt, whose access road may be seen on the left. The road under the arch leads to Ynys Hywel Countryside Centre, where there is a camping barn (see 'Transport and Facilities' section)

David James Photography (Sussex)

Until the outbreak of World War I, the Sirhowy Valley was very prosperous and the local railway carried a steady stream of coal and general freight. By 1910, the Tredegar–Newport passenger service had reached seven return workings per weekday, supplemented by a variety of shorter local journeys. There was also a healthy excursion traffic centred on Easter, Whitsun and August, plus a considerable number of colliers' trains – seventeen per day during the war itself. The distance that local people were prepared to travel on railway excursions is remarkable; most of the destinations were in the north of England, with some trains going as far as Glasgow or Edinburgh. Unfortunately, the war marked a turning point in the fortunes of this, as so many other Welsh branch lines. By the 1930s, rival bus services were taking much of the local passenger traffic and only the summer Saturday excursions attracted significant loadings. The story could be seen in the gradually reducing length of the trains: five, then four and finally two coaches each. After World War II, even the second coach was removed and the remaining, solitary vehicle would often be seen trundling through the valley behind an 0–8–0 tender engine or 0–8–4 tank – extravagant motive power for the paltry amount of traffic.

The main accident on the line occurred during the inter-war period in August 1933, when a light engine and brake van travelling north from Nine Mile Point collided with the 9.05 p.m. Newport–Tredegar service near Bird in Hand Junction. The fault appeared to lay with the signalman at Nine Mile Point No. 2 Box, who apparently sent the light engine on without transmitting any bell codes to the next box up the line. The accident telescoped together the last two coaches of the passenger train, injuring over fifty passengers and the guard. Fortunately, their injuries were not serious as the light engine was not travelling at speed. In his monograph on the line, W.W. Tasker recounts that one passenger who escaped was relieved to discover that the second engine 'was of the light type and not the heavy', which goes to show that railway terminology confused the public then as now.

With nationalization in 1948, the Sirhowy branch became part of the Western Region of British Railways. The ABC Railway Guide for August 1953 still showed a respectable service, but the crunch came in 1955 when BR decided to terminate the majority of branch services at Risca. While a sensible economy, this imposed upon passengers the inconvenience of a change and a wait for a connection – hardly an inducement to foresake the direct service offered by the buses. A few colliers' trains continued until 1957–8, but some of these were classified as 'Q' trains which only ran as required. Few could have been surprised when BR announced that passenger services between Nantybwch and Risca would be withdrawn on 13 June 1960. As there was no Sunday service, the last trains actually ran on Saturday 11 June.

After withdrawal of the passenger trains, the Sirhowy branch saw relatively little activity, a condition exacerbated by closure of the collieries at Nine Mile Point and Wyllie in 1964 and 1968 respectively. The line north of Bird in Hand Junction (near Gelligroes) closed in stages between 1960 and 1969, with the remainder following on 2 May 1970. When it was open, many historians and travellers commented on the scenic beauty of the valley through which it passed. It is fortunate indeed that some of these trackside views can still be enjoyed today.

The Line Today

After closure, the trackbed from Crosskeys to Gelligroes was purchased by Gwent County Council for a new road scheme, but the authority agreed to let the route be used as an informal recreation area until this was built. However, after a number of years, the road scheme was abandoned and the line passed to Gwent County Planning Department, which began developing it for formal recreational use. With help from Islwyn Borough Council and the Forestry Commission, which owned areas of adjoining land, the old railway was gradually transformed into a properly constituted trail with ancillary facilities such as a car park, visitors' centre, children's play area and woodland walks. It was officially designated the 'Sirhowy Valley Country Park' in 1987.

The Walk (4½ miles)

Under normal circumstances, I would recommend doing this walk downhill, i.e. from Gelligroes to Crosskeys. However, the end of the route at Gelligroes is easily missed and, for this reason alone, it is best to start at Crosskeys.

The trail begins just west of a roundabout on the A467 Crumlin–Newport road at GR 214914; the large sign to 'Sirhowy Valley Country Park' cannot be missed. Railway archaeologists will soon realize that the narrow lane leading to the country park is built on the old trackbed, as is the first mile of the dual carriageway to Newport which heads off in the opposite direction.

Fortunately, the roar of the traffic is soon forgotten as one proceeds along the lane. The former railway was cut into the valley side, so there is a steep cutting on the left and an equally steep drop to the Sirhowy River on the

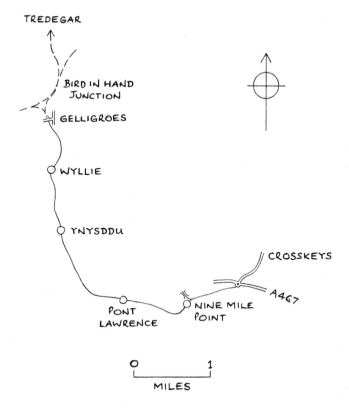

TREDEGAR

BIRD IN HAND
JUNCTION

GELLIGROES

WYLLIE

YNYSDDU

CROSSKEYS

A467

NINE MILE
POINT

PONT
LAWRENCE

O   1

MILES

Sirhowy Valley Country Park

right. The country park visitor centre is situated at GR 210913, just after an old ganger's hut built into the side of the cutting. The modern windows, new roof and recently cleaned stonework make the building difficult to date, but it is in fact a former crossing-keeper's cottage. Its occupant operated the gates over the old parish road, which is now little more than a rough track leading from the river up on to the mountainside. The house is known as Full Moon Cottage after the Full Moon public house which stood next door on the east side. All that remains of the pub today is a few stone walls between the parish road and the old permanent way. The pub gained its clientele from the rows of cottages which lined the railway, but these too have long since been demolished. Apart from the modern visitor centre, this settlement has vanished almost as thoroughly as many lost medieval villages.

Continuing along the trail, the site of Nine Mile Point station is reached at GR 203911. This area has now been attractively landscaped, with a low

Very few buildings remain from the Sirhowy Railway or its successors in the lower part of the Sirhowy Valley, so it is pleasing to discover this old gangers' hut near the visitor centre for the modern country park. Huts such as this must have provided welcome shelter for nineteenth century railwaymen, whose employers often paid scant regard to their physical comfort and sometimes even their safety

David James Photography (Sussex)

stone wall making even the car park look presentable. The children's play area on the left marks the site of the former station buildings, while further along on the right, a grassy track leading to the river marks the course of the former Penllwyn Tramroad. This was built between 1821 and 1824, but the section here was relaid as a standard gauge railway shortly after 1902. The work was carried out by Burnyeat Brown & Co., which needed a rail connection to its new pit (Nine Mile Point Colliery) on the other side of the valley. The river was crossed by a fine tramway bridge at GR 203911, which had to be reinforced by an 'arch within an arch' to take the extra weight of the frequent coal trains. (The bridge survives to this day and provides the logo for the modern country park.) Trains ceased to use this crossing in 1908, when a new bridge was opened half a mile upstream.

The new connection to Nine Mile Point Colliery is reached at GR 196911; the site is identified by a sign reading 'No. 1 Box', which refers to Nine Mile Point No. 1 signal-box. This controlled access to a double track line across the valley built by Burnyeat Brown & Co. and opened on 16 March 1908. The start of the line can still be traced, but the bridge over the river has been demolished and the colliery replaced by a modern industrial estate.

Full Moon Cottage is now the visitor and information centre for the modern Sirhowy Valley Country Park, but in years gone by it housed the crossing keeper who looked after the gates on the parish road from Crosskeys to Machen. While this town is little over a mile away as the crow flies, the parish road climbs nearly 1000 ft over Mynydd Machen to get there. No wonder it has an overgrown and disused look about it today!

David James Photography (Sussex)

The site of Pont Lawrence Halt is reached at GR 191912, although there is no trace of the station or its buildings. As one gazes around the silvan scene, it is difficult to imagine what persuaded the railway to provide a station here; the purpose was presumably to serve Cwmfelinfach, a settlement of modest size on the opposite side of the valley. This is reached by a narrow lane which at GR 186914 passes Capel-y-Babell, the memorial chapel to the Welsh poet Islwyn. Islwyn was born William Thomas on 3 April 1832. One might expect him to have had an artistic background but his father, Morgan Thomas, was the mineral agent for the Penllwyn Tramroad, while William himself worked until 1857 in the engineer's office at a mine in Pontypridd. Such was the extent to which industry and transport dominated life in the valleys.

After Pont Lawrence Halt, the railway curves around to the north, offering glimpses through the trees of the neat terraces of Cwmfelinfach on the far side of the valley. The site of Ynysddu station is reached at GR 178926 but, again, no trace remains of the platform or buildings; only the lane to the village gives the game away. A few yards later, the railway finally leaves the broadleaved woodland it has followed all the way from Full Moon Cottage and reaches an open stretch of the valley with good views to the north. This area was once dominated by Wyllie Colliery, but the workings have long been disused and the spoil heap lowered and landscaped. In fact, part of the spoil heap covers the old trackbed and the modern trail skirts around it to the east before regaining the formation at the site of Wyllie Halt (GR 176937).

As with so many stations in the Welsh valleys, nothing remains to indicate that Wyllie Halt ever existed, although it features prominently enough in local history. During a labour dispute led by the South Wales Miners' Federation in 1935, a train carrying non-Federation miners back to Merthyr Tydfil was stoned nearby. At the time, 2,000 local Federation men were conducting a 'staydown strike' and refusing to return to the surface. Those at Nine Mile Point Colliery, where the strike started, stayed underground for a total of 177 hours.

The modern trail finishes at Wyllie and joins the road leading uphill to the Islwyn Arms (closed in September 1993) and a useful general store; the access point is marked by a rusty steel barrier. Just beyond this on the right-hand side of the road, a subway passes beneath the old railway, leading downhill to a footbridge over the Sirhowy River and Pontgam Terrace beyond. Evidently, the railway wanted to attract as much traffic to the halt as possible.

Although the official trail ends at Wyllie, the railway can be followed for another ½ mile to Gelligroes; indeed, a proposal has been made to extend the path here in due course. A local footpath runs nearby, but locals have taken to using the trackbed rather than this for their journeys. This short section is not without interest and, having escaped any kind of clearance or restoration, forms quite a haven for wildlife. Rosebay willow-herb, scabious and harebells add colour to the walk, while gaps in the trees afford long views of the valley southwards to Ynysddu. About half way along, the path leaves the trackbed and runs alongside it, giving walkers the chance to view the stonework with which the railway company faced its low embankment. The path reaches Gelligroes at GR 176947 at the site of a demolished bridge; turn right here for the A4048 and buses back to Crosskeys.

The railway can be traced for another couple of hundred yards past the Half Way House pub but, after that, the route is severed by the course of a new road. In years gone by, the line forked here with separate branches running west to Ystrad Mynach and north to Tredegar. The connection to Ystrad Mynach ran over the sixteen-arch Hengoed Viaduct, which still stands at the eastern edge of the town. The Tredegar line was even more interesting, for it ran via a complicated junction at Pontllanfraith (Bird in Hand Junction), whereby it was possible for trains to join the GWR's steeply graded Neath–Pontypool line, the highlight of which was the spectacular

Crumlin Viaduct. This line closed in 1964 but, although the viaduct was scheduled for preservation, it received no maintenance after closure and had to be dismantled in 1967. A small replica was constructed in 1992 and exhibited at the Ebbw Vale National Garden Festival.

Further Explorations

Apart from the Sirhowy Railway, the main industrial route in this area with recreational potential is the Monmouthshire Canal. The main line of this waterway ran from Newport to Pontymoile (11 miles) where it made an end-on connection with the Brecknock & Abergavenny Canal (see Chapter 9), but there was also a heavily engineered branch from a point just south of Malpas to Crumlin (11 miles also). Although closed to navigation, the branch runs along the east side of Crosskeys and comes within ¾ mile of the start of the Sirhowy Valley Country Park. It is well worth exploring, for large parts of the route are still in water and the local authority has recently upgraded substantial sections of the towpath. If you are short of time, join the canal at Risca (there are several signs to it from the B4591) and head south. You will be rewarded with the sight of several fine canal bridges complete with antique signs and, at Rogerstone, a breathtaking collection of locks which raised the canal 168 ft in ½ mile. Although abandoned in 1962, these are now a scheduled ancient monument and form the centrepiece of the Fourteen Locks Canal Centre, which also includes a picnic area and display telling the history of the canal. The centre is open from Thursdays to Mondays between Easter and October; admission is free.

Sections of the canal's main line have also survived, and Torfaen Borough Council has recently upgraded the towpath between Malpas and Cwmbran into a cycle trail. At Cwmbran, the cycleway continues alongside the A4051 (Cwmbran Drive) before picking up the trackbed of the disused freight line from Llantarnam Junction to Blaenavon, which finally closed on 3 May 1980. This long-lasting BR branch was actually a combination of various older lines originating from the Newport & Pontypool, Monmouthshire and London & North Western railways – a complicated route indeed. At the time of writing, the trackbed has been converted into a cycle trail between Sebastopol and Pontypool (1½ miles), and Wainfelin and Talywain (3 miles). It is no accident that these routes run on a south–north axis, for the council intends eventually to link them into a continuous Newport to Abergavenny Cycleway.

Moving back to the Sirhowy Valley, Islwyn Borough Council is well aware of the recreational potential of other disused railways there and is currently negotiating to purchase the Sirhowy Valley line between Rock and Hollybush (4 miles). It is also interested in Hall's Road (Crosskeys to Markham Colliery, closed 1989) but admits that proposals to create a recreational trail here are unlikely to be implemented in the near future as the line has reverted to private ownership. Finally, it hopes to create a section of the Newport to Swansea Cycleway in the borough; this would see the present Sirhowy Valley route extended beyond Gelligroes and on to Ystrad Mynach, crossing the splendid viaduct at Maesycymmer. Time will tell.

Transport and Facilities

Maps: Ordnance Survey: Landranger Series Sheet 171

Buses: Glyn Williams Travel, Risca House, Waunfawr Gardens,
            Crosskeys, Gwent, NP1 7AL
            Telephone: Crosskeys (0495) 270489

            Red & White, Crosskeys Depot, Risca Road,
            Crosskeys, Gwent, NP1 7BT
            Telephone: Crosskeys (0495) 270303

            Gwent County Council, Planning & Economic Development,
            County Hall, Cwmbran, Gwent, NP44 2XF
            Telephone: Cwmbran (0633) 832478 (direct line)

            Glyn Williams and Red & White operate the Sirhowy Valley
            route jointly, with Rhondda Buses (0443 682671) taking over
            the late night services on Sundays and Bank Holiday Mondays.

Trains: British Rail Telephone Enquiry Bureau
            Telephone: Cardiff (0222) 228000

Camping: Sirhowy Valley Country Park includes a camping barn which is
            situated about 1 mile south of Cwmfelinfach on the A4048.
            This is very cheap and provides basic accommodation for up to
            eight people. For further details, contact:

            Ynys Hywel Countryside Centre, Cwmfelinfach,
            Crosskeys, Gwent, NP1 7JX
            Telephone: Crosskeys (0495) 200113

Like much of South Wales, the Sirhowy Valley is provided with a good bus service. There is only one route through the lower part of the valley (currently numbered 56), which runs from Newport to Blackwood and beyond via Crosskeys, Cwmfelinfach and Ynysddu. The basic weekday service operates every 30 minutes, although this extends to every hour on Sundays, Bank Holiday Mondays and weekday evenings. These buses run until after 10 p.m. daily.

Despite being fairly well populated, the area's supply of pubs has thinned out somewhat in recent years. The Islwyn Arms, once a convenient pub just off the trail at Wyllie, has now closed and several others in the area look as if they are struggling to make ends meet. The government deserves no thanks for its 'reforms' of the licensed trade, which have led to closures like this throughout the country. The best place to stop for refreshments is Cwmfelinfach near Pont Lawrence Halt, where Samuel Smith's will be found in evidence – all the way from Tadcaster, North Yorkshire. Mind you, this railway path is fairly short so anyone who wanders off to the pub half way along is being very decadent.

APPENDIX A

Useful Addresses

David Archer, The Pentre, Kerry, Newtown, Powys, SY16 4PD. Telephone: Newtown (0686) 670382. Supplier of second-hand maps.

The Branch Line Society, 73 Norfolk Park Avenue, Sheffield, South Yorkshire, S2 2RB.

British Waterways Board, The Wharf, Govilon, Abergavenny, Gwent, NP7 9NY. Telephone: Abergavenny (0873) 830328. Ring to obtain permission to cycle along the towpath of the Monmouthshire & Brecon Canal.

Camra Ltd., The Campaign for Real Ale, 34 Alma Road, St. Albans, Hertfordshire, AL1 3BW. Telephone: St. Albans (0727) 867201. Apart from the national Good Beer Guide, also publishes a useful range of local pub guides.

Cyclists Touring Club, 69 Meadrow, Godalming, Surrey, GU7 3HS. Telephone: Godalming (0483) 417217.

Inland Waterways Association, 114 Regents Park Road, London, NW1 8UQ. Telephone: 071 586 2510/2556.

Merthyr & Cynon Groundwork Trust, Fedw Hir, Llwydcoed, Aberdare, Mid Glamorgan, CF44 0DX. Telephone: Aberdare (0685) 883880. Publishes set of free sectional maps of the Taff Trail.

Ordnance Survey, Romsey Road, Maybush, Southampton, Hampshire, SO9 4DH. Telephone: Southampton (0703) 792000.

Railway Ramblers, Membership Secretary, 27 Sevenoaks Road, Crofton Park, London, SE4 1RA. The specialist club for exploring abandoned railways on foot.

Ramblers' Association, 1/5 Wandsworth Road, London, SW8 2XX. Telephone: 071 582 6878.

Sustrans Ltd., 35 King Street, Bristol, BS1 4DZ. Telephone: Bristol (0272) 268893. A charitable company which constructs safe off-road routes for cyclists and pedestrians – the main builder of railway paths in the UK.

APPENDIX B

Official Railway Walks

The following list has been assembled from a variety of sources, including personal inspection, information from local authorities and, to a lesser extent, other publications. Time did not permit a visit to every route, so there may be a few mistakes and omissions – hopefully very few, but details of corrections would be appreciated nonetheless. Also, please bear in mind that conversion work on some of the lines may not yet be complete: there is frequently a delay between a local authority acquiring a line and converting it for public use. As a general rule, only routes of 2 or more miles have been included, although some shorter routes are listed – especially if there are proposals to extend them.

If you wish to trace old railway lines in detail, two invaluable publications are *Railway Rights of Way* by Rhys ab Elis and *The Archaeology of an Early Railway System: The Brecon Forest Tramroads* by Stephen Hughes (see Bibliography).

Key to Abbreviations

Users: Type of Path:
C=Cyclists   DR=Disused Railway
H=Horse Riders   DT=Disused Tramway
W=Walkers   FP=Footpath

Suitability for Prams, Pushchairs and Wheelchairs:
    A=Usable throughout
    B=Usable in places
    C=Generally unsuitable
    N=Route not yet open
    X=Route not inspected

Clwyd

Corwen–Cynwyd: C, H, W, DR, 2 miles, N/X
 SJ 070433–SJ 053413
 Intended for conversion into a bridleway; the first half mile south of
 Corwen is already in place. See also note below.
Greenfield–Holywell Town: W, DR, 1¼ miles, C
 SJ 197774–SJ 187760
Minera Lime Works–New Brighton: W, DR, 1 mile, X
 SJ 259519–SJ 276507
Prestatyn–Marian Mill:
(1) Prestatyn–Dyserth: W, DR, 2¾ miles, B
 SJ 063829–SJ 063793
(2) Dyserth–Marian Mill: W, DR, ½ mile, C
 SJ 063793–SJ 072792
 The most forgotten of disused railways, this privately-built formation
 was never actually laid with track. It is most easily found at the
 Dyserth end.
Towyn–A55 nr. Faenol Bach: W, DR, 3 miles, X
 SH 990794–SH 983762

Note: Clwyd County Council advises that the following routes have right of
way claims pending and may become available shortly:

Cynwyd–Llandrillo: W, DR, 2 miles, N/X
Trevor–Bryn Howel: W, DR, 1½ miles, N/X

Wrexham Maelor Borough Council has also created some permissive
railway walks, although all of them were less than two miles long at the time
of publication.

Dyfed

Aberaeron: C, W, DR, ½ mile, X
 SN 462620–SN 469611
Aberaeron–Llanaeron Estate: W, DR, 1¾ miles, N (proposed)
 SN 469611–SN489597
Cynheidre–Cross Hands: W, DR, 6 miles, X
 SN 496082–SN 559132
 Judging from the OS map, access to the southern end of this route is
 difficult.
Johnston–Neyland: W, DR, 4½ miles, B
 SM 937102–SM 967048
King's Moor–Thomas Chapel: W, DT, 2¼ miles, C
 SN 122067–SN 103089

Maesllyn Farm–Allt-ddu–Cors Caron: W, DR, 1½ miles, X
SN 695630–SN 704648
Parc y Llong–Cwm Mawr: W, DR, 7¼ miles, X
SN 437065–SN 530127
Stepaside–Saundersfoot–Ridgeway: W, DT, 3 miles, B
SN 138077–SN 137048–SN 127053
Starts in a caravan park. If in difficulty, ask for directions at Stepaside Visitors Centre. The section between Wiseman's Bridge and Saundersfoot includes three tunnels on the Pembrokeshire Coast Path.

Note: Dyfed CC has not taken much interest in reusing disused railways and some of the above routes could be difficult. Until recently, the Cynheidre–Cross Hands and Parc y Llong–Cwm Mawr routes were in use as operational railways. The council maintains that a right of way exists alongside these lines (a view corroborated by the Ordnance Survey), probably originating from their early days as tramroads.

Glamorgan, Mid
Abertridwr–Nant yr Aber: C, W, DR, 1½ miles, X
ST 123890–ST 141879
Part of the former Rhymney Railway's Senghenydd branch. An extension is proposed northwards to Senghenydd which will lengthen the route to 3 miles.
Bargoed–Parc Cwm Darran: C, W, DR, 4½ miles, B
SO 149003–SO 110043
Cefn Cribwr–Kenfig Hill–Frog Pond: C, W, DR, 2¼ miles, A
SS 854834–SS 833829–SS 841819
Dare Valley Country Park:
(1) Cwmaman–Cwmdare: C, W, DR, 3¾ miles, X
SO 003995–SN 980028
Part of the GWR Cwmaman branch.
(2) Cwmdare–Gadlys: C, W, DR, 1 mile, X
SN 980028–SN 998026
Part of a Taff Vale Railway branch from Dare Valley Junction to Bwllfa Dare Colliery.
Hirwaun–Penderyn: C, W, DR, 2½ miles, X
SN 959061–SN 951085
Hirwaun–Aberdare: C, W, DT, 4 miles, X
SN 965052–SO 005028
Part of the Hirwaun-Abernant Tramroad, last used in 1900. The first half mile at the Hirwaun end survives in very good condition, complete with stone sleepers, passing loops, boundary hedges and culverts.

Llwydcoed–Cwmbach: W, DR, 2½ miles, X
  SN 989051–SO 024027
  Part of the former GWR line from Gelli Tarw Junction to Merthyr
  Tydfil, terminating near the southern end of the 1½ mile Merthyr
  Tunnel (details supplied by Cynon Valley Borough Council).
Nantymoel–Brynmenyn: C, W, DR, 6½ miles, A
  SS 933930–SS 905848
  Stopped about 1 mile short of Brynmenyn in late 1993 but an extension
  to the village is planned. Note, however, that an application for mineral
  extraction rights is pending and this could effectively block the cycle trail
  by reviving the southern end of the railway. Connecting routes are
  proposed from Brynmenyn to Blaengarw, Bridgend and Tondu.
The Taff Trail:
(1) Abercynon–Pontygwaith: C, W, DT, 2½ miles, B
  ST 085949–ST 081978
  Part of the historic Pennydarren Tramroad, including two stone-built
  single-span tramway bridges at Edwardsville which are now scheduled
  ancient monuments.
(2) Pontsticill–Cefn Coed: C, W, DR, 3 miles, A
  SO 061106–SO 032080
(3) Pontypridd–Castell Coch: C, W, mainly DR, 7 miles, B
  ST 086892–ST 129836
  Comprises sections of the Alexandra (Newport & South Wales) Docks
  & Railway, the Barry Railway and the Rhymney Railway. The surface
  on the railway sections is excellent, but the link from the Rhymney
  Railway to Castell Coch involves a ludicrously steep descent which is
  totally unsuitable for prams, wheelchairs, etc.
Trehafod–Maesycoed, Pontypridd: C, W, partly DR, 1½ miles, X
  ST 043910–ST 064902
  Uses part of the Barry Railway from Trehafod to Tonteg Junction but
  avoids the trackbed at the Trehafod end in order to circumnavigate a
  demolished river bridge.

Glamorgan, South

No substantial railway paths yet, but 8 miles of the Three Castles cycle trail
are complete. This shares the same route as the Taff Trail and currently
runs from Cardiff to Castell Coch; an extension to Caerphilly is planned
which is likely to use the disused Rhymney Railway between Nantgarw and
Caerphilly. The Three Castles route includes part of the little-known
Melingriffith Tramway:

Tongwynlais–Melingriffith: C, W, DT, 1½ miles, A
  ST 131816–ST 143804

Glamorgan, West

Afan Valley Country Park:
(1) Cymmer–Blaengwynfi: C, W, DR, 2 miles, B
    SS 860962–SS 885968
(2) Cymmer–Glyncorrwg–North Rhondda: C, W, DR, 3½ miles, B
    SS 860964–SS 874992–SN 887005
(3) Pontrhydyfen–Efail-fâch: C, W, DR, 1 mile, A
    SS 793940–SS 787954
(4) Pontrhydyfen–Abercregan–Cymmer: C, W, DR, 5½ miles, B
    SS 800942–SS 850966–SS 860964
(5) Pontrhydyfen–Cynonville–Cymmer: C, W, DR, 5½ miles, A
    SS 800942–SS 821952–SS 860962
Briton Ferry–nr. Gelli-gaer: W, DR, 1½ miles, X
    SS 743949–SS 766952
Bryn–Goytre: W, DR, 3¼ miles, X
    SS 819920–SS 781897
Clydach–Cwm Clydach: W, DT, 3 miles, X
    SN 687010–SN 688052
    The Lower Clydach Tramway, latterly an NCB branch line.
Gorseinon–Grovesend: C, W, DR, 1½ miles, A
    SS 595986–SN 598010
    In the past, motorcyclists have been a nuisance on this trail.
    Complaints should be addressed to the Chief Executive, Civic Centre,
    Penllergaer, Swansea, SA4 1GH.
Onllwyn–Ystradgynlais: H, W, DT, 3½ miles, X
    SN 840105–SN 786098
    Part of Claypons Tramroad, now a scheduled ancient monument.
    There is no right of way over the short section from SN 795097 to
    SN 790097, but a bridleway and minor road offer a convenient detour
    to the north.
Swansea Bikepath Network:
(1) Black Pill–Gowerton: C, W, DR, 4 miles, A
    SS 619908–SS 595952
(2) Swansea Marina–Mumbles: C, W, DR, 5 miles, A
    SS 660924–SS 630875

Gwent

Crosskeys–Gelligroes: C, W, DR, 4½ miles, B
    ST 214913–ST 176947
Heads of the Valleys Line:
    The following three entries, used in conjunction with local footpaths,
    provide an almost continuous railway walk from Brynmawr to
    Llanfoist, on the western edge of Abergavenny.

(1) Brynmawr–Coed Ffyddlwn: C, W, DR, 2 miles, X
SO 197121–SO 222125
In 1993, only the first ¾ mile was open at the Brynmawr end, but an extension to Coed Ffyddlwn was proposed. Until the route is extended, parallel footpaths provide an alternative way of tracing the line.
(2) Clydach Gorge: W, FP, 3 miles, B
Access at SO 231134
Includes only a small part of the railway trackbed, but this official walk around Clydach Gorge passes Clydach station, the seven arch Clydach Viaduct and the two Clydach tunnels. Connects with section (1) and the Llam-march Railroad, built in 1795 to serve the Clydach Ironworks. Be warned that there are some steep climbs and descents. Leaflet available from the Tourism Officer, Blaenau Gwent Borough Council, Civic Centre, Ebbw Vale, Gwent, NP3 6XB. Tel. Ebbw Vale (0495) 350555.
(3) Gilwern–Govilon–Llanfoist: C, W, DR, 3½ miles, B
SO 251138–SO 268137–SO 292137
Pontypool–Sebastopol: C, W, DR, 1½ miles, X
SO 288003–ST 295976
Redbrook–Whitebrook: W, DR, 2¼ miles, X
SO 536101–SO 537068
Part of the Wye Valley Walk, including a GWR river bridge at Redbrook.
Wainfelin–Talywain: C, W, DR, 3 miles, X
SO 275017–SO 264023

The Heads of the Valleys Line, Pontypool–Sebastopol and Wainfelin–Talywain are all part of the proposed Newport to Abergavenny Cycleway.

Gwynedd

Bangor–Glasinfryn: C, W, DR, 2¼ miles, X
SH 592721–SH 587692
Bangor and Bethesda were linked by two railways: a standard gauge LNWR branch line, and a privately owned narrow gauge line that ran from Lord Penrhyn's quarries at Bethesda to Porth Penrhyn on the coast. This cycle trail uses the latter.
Beddgelert–Ynys Fer-las: W, DR, 3 miles, C
SH 589474–SH 601435
Caernarfon–Bryncir: C, W, DR, 12½ miles, B
SH 480626–SH 479447
Dolgellau–Morfa Mawddach: C, W, DR, 7¾ miles, B
SH 714183–SH 628141

Powys

Elan Valley (Caban Coch–Craig Goch): W, DR, 5½ miles, C
    SN 926647–SN 895687

Llangurig–Skew Bridge: W, DR, 1¼ miles, X
    SN 909799–SN 927800
    Part of the northern section of the ill-fated Manchester & Milford
    Railway which was built and laid with double track but never opened.
    Only a single freight train to Llangurig ever ran over the line.

Onllwyn–Ystradgynlais: H, W, DT, 3½ miles, X
    SN 840105–SN 786098
    See entry under West Glamorgan

Talybont on Usk–Torpantau Tunnel: W, DR, 6 miles, B
    SO 108210–SO 057171

Talybont on Usk–Ffos y Wern: W, DT, 7 miles, C
    SO 116226–SO 108152

BIBLIOGRAPHY

General

Awdry, Christopher, *Encyclopaedia of British Railway Companies*, Patrick Stephens Ltd, 1990

Barrie, D.S.M., *A Regional History of the Railways of Great Britain, Volume 12: South Wales*, David & Charles, 1980

Bradshaw's July 1922 Railway Guide (reprint), David & Charles, 1985

Baughan, Peter E., *A Regional History of the Railways of Great Britain, Volume 11: North and Mid Wales* (2nd edition), David & Charles, 1991

Christiansen, Rex, *Forgotten Railways, Volume 4: North and Mid Wales*, David & Charles, 1976

Christiansen, Rex, *Forgotten Railways, Volume 11: Severn Valley and Welsh Border*, David & Charles, 1988

Daniels, Gerald, and Dench, Les, *Passengers No More* (3rd edition), Ian Allan, 1980

Hughes, Stephen, *The Archaeology of an Early Railway System: The Brecon Forest Tramroads*, Royal Commission on Ancient Historical Monuments in Wales, 1990

Page, James, *Forgotten Railways, Volume 8: South Wales* (2nd edition), David & Charles, 1988

Page, James, *Rails in the Valleys*, David & Charles, 1989

Ransom, P.J.G., *The Archaeology of Railways*, World's Work Ltd, 1981

Railway Gazetteers and Atlases

Conolly, W. Philip, *British Railways Pre-Grouping Atlas and Gazetteer* (5th edition), Ian Allan, 1972

Elis, Rhys ab, *Railway Rights of Way*, plus 3 Supplements, Branch Line Society, 1985-1989

Jowett, Alan, *Jowett's Railway Atlas*, Patrick Stephens Ltd, 1989

Wignall, C.J., *Complete British Railways Maps and Gazetteer, 1825–1985* (2nd edition), Oxford Publishing Co., 1985

Chapter 1: The Clwyd Coast

Goodall, Stephen P., *The Prestatyn and Dyserth Branch Line*, Oakwood Press, 1986

Thompson, Trefor, *The Prestatyn and Dyserth Railway*, 1978

Various, *The Prestatyn-Dyserth Walkway*, Rhuddlan Borough Council, 1992

There are currently no monographs on the Holywell Town branch. The best account appears in Peter Baughan's volume in the Regional History series (see above).

Chapter 2: Lôn Eifion

Blencowe, M., 'The Welsh Highland Railway', article in *Railway Ramblings*, January 1992

Dunn, J.M., 'The Afonwen Line', two-part article in *Railway Magazine*, September/October 1958

Kidner, R.W., *The Narrow Gauge Railways of Wales*, 1972

Lee, Charles E., *The Welsh Highland Railway*, David & Charles

Rear, W.G., *LMS Branch Lines in North Wales, Volume 1: Bangor to Afonwen, Llanberis and Nantlle*, Wild Swan Publishing, 1986

Chapter 3: The Mawddach Estuary

Christiansen, Rex, and Miller, R.W., *The Cambrian Railways* (2 Volumes), David & Charles, 1967 and 1968

Hambly, Mark, et al., *Railways of the Wnion Valley and the Mawddach Estuary*, Llangollen Railway Society, 1991

Chapter 4: The Elan Valley

Christiansen, Rex, and Miller, R.W., *The Cambrian Railways, Volume II: 1889–1968*, David & Charles, 1968

Judge, Colin, *The Elan Valley Railway*, Oakwood Press, 1987

Chapter 5: The Dyfed Coast

Price, M.R.C., *The Saundersfoot Railway* (4th edition), Oakwood Press, 1989

There are currently no monographs on the Johnston–Neyland line. The best account appears in D.S.M. Barrie's volume in the *Regional History* series (see above).

Chapter 6: The Swansea Bikepath Network

Gabb, Gerald, *The Life and Times of the Swansea and Mumbles Railway*, D. Brown & Sons, 1987
Lee, Charles E., *The Swansea and Mumbles Railway*, Oakwood Press, 1977
Mumbles Railway Society, *The Mumbles Railway: The World's First Passenger Railway* (2nd edition), Mumbles Railway Society, 1985
Smith, D.J., *Shrewsbury to Swansea*, Town & Country Press, 1971

Chapter 7: The Afan Valley

Smith, Clive, *Bygone Railways of the Afan*, Alun Books, 1982

There are one or two inaccuracies in this small volume, but it contains some interesting details. Surprisingly, there is no other monograph on railways in the Afan Valley.

Chapter 8: The Ogmore Valley

Barrie, D.S.M., 'The Porthcawl Branch', article in *Railway Magazine*, March 1954
Barrie, D.S.M., 'Railways of the Bridgend District', article in *Railway Magazine*, July 1955

Judge, C.W., *The Porthcawl Branch*, Oakwood Press, 1994
Richards, S., *The Llynfi & Ogmore Railway*, Morgannwg, 1977

Most of the literature on the Llynfi & Ogmore Railway concentrates on the Porthcawl branch, whose interesting history has preoccupied writers for over 40 years. By comparison, the line to Nantymoel has been neglected.

Chapter 9: The Taff Trail

Barry, D.S.M., *The Brecon and Merthyr Railway* (4th impression), Oakwood Press, 1980
Vinter, Jeff, *The Taff Trail Official Guide*, Alan Sutton Publishing, 1993

Chapter 10: The Darran Valley

Barry, D.S.M., *The Brecon and Merthyr Railway* (4th impression), Oakwood Press, 1980
Barry, D.S.M., *The Rhymney Railway*, Oakwood Press

Chapter 11: Sirhowy Valley Country Park

Tasker, W.W., *Railways in the Sirhowy Valley* (2nd edition), Oakwood Press, 1992

Canals

Gladwin, D.D. and J.M., *Canals of the Welsh Valleys and Their Tramroads*, Oakwood Press
Hadfield, Charles, *British Canals: An Illustrated History* (7th edition), David & Charles, 1984
Hadfield, Charles, *Canals of South Wales and the Border* (2nd edition), David & Charles, 1967
Russell, Ronald, *Lost Canals of England and Wales* (2nd edition), David & Charles, 1988

INDEX